P9-CQX-798

Play
IN THE LIVES
OF CHILDREN

Cosby S. Rogers and
Janet K. Sawyers

NATIONAL ASSOCIATION FOR THE
EDUCATION OF YOUNG CHILDREN

Washington, D.C.

Photocredits:
Subject & Predicates, viii, 60, 65, 74, 87, 100; Ellen Galinsky, 6; Rich Rosenkoetter, 14; Jim Cronk (© 1988), 18; Faith Bowlus, 26; Francis Wardle, 47, 115; Jack Hillwig (© 1983), 53; Doris Wilder, 68; Robert J. Bennett, 92; Marietta Lynch, 98; Peggy O'Neil Banning (© 1988), 103; Bob Taylor, 110

Cover photographs:
Faith Bowlus, Bob Taylor (© 1988); Subject & Predicates, Jim Bradshaw (© 1988)

Authors' names are listed alphabetically. Each author contributed equally to the manuscript.

National Association for the Education of Young Children
1509 16th Street, NW
Washington, DC 20036-1426
202-232-8777 or 800-424-2460
Website: http://www.naeyc.org

The National Association for the Education of Young Children (NAEYC) attempts through its publications program to provide a forum for discussion of major issues and ideas in our field. We hope to provoke thought and promote professional growth. The views expressed or implied are not necessarily those of the Association. NAEYC wishes to thank the authors, who donated much time and effort to develop this book as a contribution to our profession.

Library of Congress Catalog Card Number: 87-062314
ISBN Catalog Number: 0-935989-09-9
NAEYC #301

Printed in the United States of America

Table of Contents

96789

Introduction

Why is play important?

Our society has become increasingly complex, competitive, and fast-paced. As a result, children's spontaneous play is being replaced with structured activities, both at home and in school. This practice reflects an earnest desire by parents and teachers to provide what is best for the child. We all want children to compete successfully in our complex, hurry-up world.

Unfortunately, structured, adult-directed activities such as worksheets and drill are *not* likely to help children make the most of their childhood. This approach to education will not give children the skills and attitudes they need to be able to adapt to the demands of the future. Such rigid activities may even prevent children from enjoying and making the most of their personal and professional lives. In fact, this hurried, structured, work-oriented approach is based on several *unwarranted and faulty beliefs:*

- earlier is better

- children are not interested in learning unless they receive rewards

- success and winning are more important than effort

- teacher-directed work is the most efficient way for children to learn

- play has little value

If structured, adult-directed activities are not the most effective way for children to learn and develop, then what is? Self-paced, child-controlled play is the best way for children to make the most of their lives!

On the surface, children's play looks deceptively simple. In fact, there are many different kinds of play in which children engage throughout childhood. Play touches on every aspect of development and learning. Therefore, any program that claims to offer a curriculum that is more than "just play" is ignoring what many researchers and theorists have found out about how young children learn.

We already know a great deal about the value of children's play, and we still have much more to discover. This book will review what we know about the intricacies of children's play. Based on that information, we will then offer some suggestions for parents, teachers, and program directors to use to encourage children's playful living, learning, and developing at home and in school. Our first step is to know what play is, and what it is not.

What is play?

Play has been defined in a variety of ways such as relaxation, surplus energy, practice, and wish fulfillment. Rubin, Fein, and Vandenberg (1983) attempted to pull together and make sense of these diverse definitions of play. What they found presents a more manageable and complete picture. These three common aspects have stood the test of time in definitions of play:

1. Children's feelings or motivation—the *disposition* of play
2. How children act when they play—the types of *behaviors*
3. Where children play—the *environment* in which play occurs

In Chapter 1 we will look more closely at what motivates children to play and therefore learn. Chapters 2 and 3 will explore different ways to look at play and how play behaviors change as children grow. We will then review, in Chapter 4, how play overlaps into all areas of children's social, emotional, physical, and cognitive development. Finally, we will pull all this knowledge together to make some recommendations about how to arrange children's play areas and select the most appropriate toys and activities as we look at the play environment in Chapters 5 and 6.

As you make your way through this fascinating glimpse into the value of children's play, you may want to learn more about the various definitions of play. We suggest you locate these references: Berlyne, 1966, 1969; Bruner, 1972; Csikszentmihalyi, 1975, 1979; Ellis, 1973; Hutt, 1976, 1979; Piaget, 1951/1962; Rubin, 1982a; Vygotsky, 1967; Weisler & McCall, 1976; as well as others you will find cited throughout the text.

Adults can provide the appropriate materials and the setting, but only the child can select the best match in which learning is most likely to occur.

Chapter one

Play Is Life
for Young Children

When all aspects of human behavior are integrated, as they are in children's play, the most can be made of life's experiences. The most significant attribute of play may well be that it unifies the mind, body, and spirit (Levy, 1978).

Play is perhaps the only human behavior that integrates and balances all aspects of human functioning. This chapter will explore what motivates children to play and what makes play children's preferred activity. We will start by looking in detail at six factors that make up what might be called the *disposition* of play, as synthesized by Rubin, Fein, and Vandenberg (1983):

1. Play is intrinsically motivated.
2. Play is relatively free of externally imposed rules.
3. Play is carried out as if the activity were real.
4. Play focuses on the process rather than any product.
5. Play is dominated by the players.
6. Play requires the active involvement of the player.

Why children want to play

Children are by nature playful. They enjoy playing, and will do so whenever they can latch onto the opportunity. Challenges intrigue them. They can concentrate for long periods to perfect a skill. Good feelings spur children on to try something new. Why do children love to play? Because play is intrinsically motivated—no one else tells them what to do or how to do it. An activity ceases to be play, and children's interest dwindles, if adults structure or even interfere inappropriately with the play.

As an intrinsically motivated behavior, play may be the most important process through which children learn to adapt to the world and become more mature. If we are to understand the value of play we must know why it is so important for play to be intrinsically motivated. A.E. Gottfried (1985) offers a fascinating summary of three theories of intrinsic motivation related to play: cognitive discrepancy, competence/mastery, and attribution.

An activity ceases to be play, and children's interest dwindles, if adults structure or even interfere inappropriately with the play.

To match the new with the known   Before we define cognitive discrepancy, let's see how the idea works in an example of children at play.

A corner of the classroom for 4-year-olds is set up as a medical office with a cot, masks, gloves, a stethoscope, note paper, and pencils. Sheroka, who is the doctor, begins to fill out a prescription pad, writing R_x and numbers for the number of days her patient is to take the medicine. Another doctor, Robbie, comes to the teacher concerned that he does not know how to spell words on the prescription. The teacher notes that the doctor's name is needed on the prescription. Robbie busily begins to fill out prescriptions with his name, and later adds other combinations of letters on his prescription pad.

Both Sheroka and Robbie selected a new activity—writing prescriptions. Each child chose to carry out that activity in a way that matched her or his skill level: Sheroka wrote R_x and numbers, while Robbie wrote his name and other familiar letters. Both children experienced cognitive discrepancy: They encountered a situation different from what they knew or had experienced. While an adult provided the opportunity for variety, the children themselves solved what is often called *the problem of the match* through play.

Children are curious. They like to explore new things. They are intrigued by the incongruous and the complex. They delight in being surprised. All of these are features of cognitive discrepancy. The idea of cognitive discrepancy can help us identify the "characteristics of play materials and play experiences that increase arousal and facilitate play" (A.E. Gottfried, 1985, p. 47).

Writing, as Sheroka and Robbie did, is a complex behavior involving a variety of motor, cognitive, and social-emotional skills. This setting enabled them to match the activity to their skills. It was pressure free. Neither child was frustrated by a task that was too simple or too difficult. Neither felt like a failure for not measuring up to the teacher's expectations or another child's abilities. What a fine example of how children benefit from self-motivated play!

How much discrepancy is effective? It appears that a moderate arousal level is most likely to lead to complex learning (Sutton-Smith, 1979). In play, children tend to select activities that offer this most effective level. An adult, on the other hand, might well cause the child anxiety by offering a task that is too difficult (perhaps asking Robbie to copy something the teacher wrote on a prescription pad) or one that is too simple and thus boring (such as suggesting Robbie write just one letter on the pad).

In play, children voluntarily elaborate and complicate the activity. If you have the chance, offer a preschool child a box of small blocks in different shapes and colors, and watch what happens. The child may devise an elaborate classification system to sort the blocks, or perhaps will build an intricate design with them. This self-motivated activity is much more valuable than asking the child to sort all the red blocks, all the green blocks, and all the yellow blocks into three piles.

Adults can provide the appropriate materials and the setting, but only the child can select the best match in which learning is most likely to occur.

In play, children voluntarily elaborate and complicate the activity.

To feel competent   According to the competence/mastery view, play is a child's way of controlling the environment. Through play children learn that they can cause things to happen or change (Piaget, 1963). Children begin to see how what they do has cause and effect, and they begin to assume responsibility for their behavior.

When people or objects are not responsive to children's actions, children give up in despair, not because of the actual severity of the situation, but because they feel they have little or no effect on it. Children learn to feel helpless when they experience events they cannot control or are led to believe they cannot control (Seligman et al., 1984). Children's self-esteem and sense of competence is affected by whether they feel they have some control over what happens to them (Connell, 1985; Harter, 1983). Children who have a strong sense of self-worth are much more likely to be well-rounded, mature individuals.

What happens when there is a conflict between adult demands and the child's need for personal control? Jessica was caught in just such a bind.

> Jessica attended two preschool programs with two very different philosophies. In one, she was told exactly how to use the materials and equipment, and told which materials she could use. In the other, she was given a choice of activities and allowed to use the materials in any safe and reasonable way.
>
> One day, her teacher at the second school found her crying. When the teacher asked what was wrong, Jessica said she did not like the school because nobody told her what to do.
>
> The teacher met with Jessica's parents, who then observed at both programs and talked with the staff. Her parents concluded that the structured environment was causing Jessica distress and removed her from that school. With help from her teacher, Jessica learned to take delight in assuming responsibility for choosing activities and using materials and equipment in a variety of ways.

How fortunate that Jessica's parents and teacher were able to see how important it is for children to feel some degree of control over their lives—to learn to make choices and to accept responsibility for those choices.

This ability to accept challenges is also a component of the competence/mastery view. Challenge can enhance children's motivation to gain even further mastery over their environment.

> Mastery is achieved one small step at a time. Play permits children to decide both the size of those steps and provides an "as if" context allowing trial and error experimentation. Though the road may be long, it leads to competent, well-adjusted and satisfying interaction with the environment. (Mann, 1984, p. 75)

Another value of play is that children can pick the level of skill and challenge with which they feel comfortable.

> Nickcolder's parents gave her swimming lessons at ages 2 and 3, but each lesson was met with resistance. By the time she was 4, she still did

not know how to swim, but did like to dabble in the water at the wading pool. Her parents then arranged private lessons with a favorite preschool teacher. With each lesson, Nickcolder grew more reluctant to return to the pool. The more external pressure put on her to learn, the more resistant she became.

By Nickcolder's fifth summer, her parents gave up their goal and decided to let her just play and be with friends in the shallow end of the pool. Soon, Nickcolder started to really enjoy playing in the water. Then she began to imitate others who could swim. Within a few days, she could swim for 6 feet.

Once again, we see how important it is for children to have a sense of control and to be able to match skills and challenges to their interests. Children who experience success are more likely not only to want to repeat the experience, but to want to take on new or more difficult challenges as well (Harter, 1978, 1981; MacTurk, Vietze, McCarthy, McQuiston, & Yarrow, 1985). Play gives them the opportunity for success.

Mastery behavior, as evidenced by Nickcolder, is characterized by being directed, selective, and persistent (White, 1959). Sometimes children persist even in the face of discouragement.

Terrance is a second grader who enjoys building things with his tool set. He makes things that require more and more skill to complete. Even though his older sisters sometimes are indifferent or laugh at his inventions, he persists in making new construction projects.

Why does Terrance persist? Because with each new creation he feels a sense of mastery for having met a new challenge. In play, children persist until they learn what can and cannot be done. Play provides a minimum of risk and penalties for mistakes. This tendency to persist appears to continue into adulthood, especially in the work of artists, musicians, and entertainers who must face the acceptance or rejection of their work, or by scientists who may spend years pursuing research for which the outcome is unknown.

On the other hand, children who frequently experience failure or frustration with tasks that are too difficult are not likely to want to pursue the activity. This is precisely the problem with many books, games, and toys that purport to mold the child into a genius, a great athlete, or a famous artist. These materials set up the parents to expect that the child can successfully carry out the activity. When the child fails or shows no interest, parents often push harder. Both child and parent become frustrated. The child learns to avoid such activities and may feel like a failure.

Children who experience success are more likely not only to want to repeat the experience, but to want to take on new or more difficult challenges as well. Play gives children the opportunity for success.

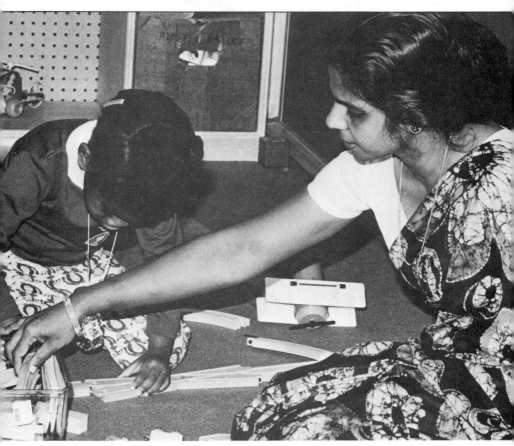

The cycle of frustration, failure, and lack of interest in learning can also result when children's early school experiences are not developmentally appropriate or when they have little or no relation to the children's interests, needs, and goals.

As adults, we are often reluctant to relinquish the control over the learning situation to children. Many of us are more comfortable when we are directly teaching than when we act as facilitators for children's play. But we must allow children to play if they are to learn.

There is no guarantee that just because children have been exposed to knowledge through direct instruction they will learn what is being taught. Children do not necessarily learn more and faster in direct instruction than in play. Even in direct instruction, children will choose whether or not to be involved and whether or not to incorporate new knowledge and skills into their own framework.

In play, children are much freer to incorporate new knowledge at their own rate and in their own way. This reduces the inevitable tension and anxiety that can inhibit learning. Play experiences "that provide the child with a sense of control and feedback contingent upon the child's own actions are likely to enhance mastery motivation" (A.E. Gottfried, 1985, p. 48).

To enjoy the activity   Children tend to find intrinsically motivated activities—play and consequently learning —inherently pleasurable (A.E. Gottfried, 1985). When children are self-motivated, they enjoy the activity for itself. Externally motivated behaviors, on the other hand, are usually carried out just to get a reward or some desirable outcome.

Here again we can see the value of play. Young children do not differentiate between play, learning, and work. When children are engaged in play, they are learning and enjoying every minute of it.

Young children's play is spontaneous. They seem to have an insatiable curiosity for learning. Parents and teachers alike lament the loss of this spontaneity and curiosity, which often begins in kindergarten or even earlier if the program is inappropriate. By the early elementary years, children's drawings all look alike. They no longer enthusiastically go off to school each morning. All too soon, tests, gold stars, awards, grades, and even money are offered in an effort to restore motivation to learn.

How does this change come about? Adults, not children's development, are responsible. Comments such as "Quit playing around and get to work" or "You may go out to play when your work is finished" teach children that learning and work are aversive activities. Using play, recess, or other intrinsically motivated activities as rewards for completing schoolwork or chores at home teaches children that learning and work require external motivation.

Praise and rewards are unnecessary to encourage intrinsically motivated behaviors (Leeper, Greene, & Nisbett, 1973). In fact, the use of rewards for such activities may undermine the child's own feelings and motives, and eventually even replace them.

Young children who are exposed to indiscriminate praise and rewards learn to rely on recognition of their activity by the important people in their lives. They are then motivated only by the dangling carrot—receiving a reward—rather than by the self-sustaining interest in the activity itself.

Children who learn to expect external rewards for every accomplishment come to rely on them to bolster their feelings of self-worth and to motivate them to achieve goals and are then often ill-prepared to handle the real world, where reinforcement for work and the responsibilities of daily life is less frequent or even nonexistent. Indeed,

> it is when we want to develop initiative, creativity, and problem-solving that praise fails us the most. To liberate these qualities in people, we need to make people feel they are free of our control. (Farson, cited in Strom, 1981, p. 97)

Furthermore, rewards or praise for less than adequate performance may indicate to the child that the performance is good enough and that there is no need to work for perfection of the ability or skill.

Maintaining children's In summarizing the research on the effects
intrinsic motivation of rewards on intrinsic motivation, A.E. Gottfried (1985) concluded that rewards have complex effects on intrinsic motivation—sometimes positive and sometimes detrimental. The key seems to be the child's view of the purpose for the activity.

All three of these views—cognitive discrepancy, competence/mastery, and attribution—are needed to explain motivation in play. At times one type may be sufficient, but at other times all three operate together, depending on the child's age and the play itself. Gottfried

---

A playful disposition toward life can carry over from childhood to adulthood.

---

argues that intrinsic motivation is an outcome of play rather than a criterion for play, and indirect support for this idea has been reported (Smith & Vollstedt, 1985).

Gottfried also believes that the child's perspective of the event is an important factor that has been overlooked. For example, learning the alphabet may be a good match and a cognitive challenge to a child, or it may be done under the pressure to achieve put on the child by peers, parents, or teachers.

Differences between adults' and children's play

From the child's point of view, play is something you don't have to do well, it is just fun (Caldwell, 1985). Until the ages of 7 or 8, children are much more interested in what they are doing (the process) rather than how it turns out (the product). It appears that children engage in play for the pleasure of the activity itself until they become relatively skilled. Then they alter the activity to create new challenges. Play offers a multitude of risk-free opportunities to match skills and challenges.

As adults, we rarely allow ourselves the luxury of engaging in real play. We tend to limit our pursuits to the things we do well, afraid to take the risk of trying something new and failing. Perhaps the closest we come to play as children know it is when we take up a new game or attempt a new craft. As beginners, we are willing to suspend or bend the rules a little, until we perfect the skill. If we win or succeed in our first attempts, we attribute it to beginner's luck. Adult play (such as bridge, tennis, or fishing) has aptly been described as having the following characteristics: not fun; lacking spontaneity; deadly serious —very literal; and focused on doing it correctly and well (Caldwell, 1985). In other words, adults tend to view play as a means to an end, whereas children ignore the end in order to explore, enjoy, and toy with the means (Fagan, 1984).

In our society, we are often in a big hurry to impose the rules of the game or a goal on young children (the end), insisting that they do it the correct way before they have had the opportunity to explore and enjoy the means to that end. Adults who wait to play games with children until they can play by the rules will miss out on a lot of pleasurable experiences for everyone.

For instance, we give children coloring books to "teach" them to stay within the lines, rather than giving them paper and crayons to let them explore the possibilities of what can be done with the materials. Children can draw their own lines, and will color them in if they wish. With coloring books, children learn failure—that they cannot draw as well as the pictures in the book are drawn. When patterns such as these are used, soon everyone's work looks just alike. How boring!

Many adults value and promote convergent thinking and perhaps even unintentionally exclude divergent play and thinking. We assume that children who can adopt the adult-oriented emphasis on goals will have an advantage in school. Instead, what we may be doing is sentencing children to a life in which they are afraid to take a risk, to explore, or to enjoy.

What is an appropriate role for adults in playing with children? Children often need adult or peer stimulation in order to sustain their play (Caldwell, 1985). Adults can keep the play light by suspending rules and patterns, thus giving children opportunity for flexibility and spontaneity. Often children's interest in play outlasts that of the adult, and at other times children may not want to play, so the pleasures will vary. Children seem to be able to sense which adults will play with them and which will not. Even infants respond to adults who are more fun (Beckwith, 1985). When you were a child, who was your favorite teacher or relative? Was it not one who was playful?

Children are actively involved

Children who are engaged in play are actively involved. Children cannot be passive recipients of play. When children's action and awareness merge, they become autonomous thinkers, not robots. The play-based curriculum values and promotes child-initiated individuality and autonomous thinking. Some have argued that these experiences do not prepare children for the expectations of formal schooling and the real world (Tizard, 1977). In this view, the real world offers little intrinsic satisfaction, is rigidly defined by someone else, and is a place where autonomy and creativity are discouraged. Even if that is an accurate, if dismal, picture of the real world, "there is an enormous difference between a correct answer produced autonomously with personal conviction and one produced heteronomously by obedience" (Kamii, 1982, p. 86).

Another argument for the value of play is that it provides the child with opportunities to develop the skills of "*active* environment-building" (Fagan, 1984). Play provides children the chance to turn passive experiences—things that have been done to them—into activity. For instance, in playing Peek-A-Boo, infants can master social situations (Beckwith, 1985). They actively play out, with pleasure, the negative feelings associated with separation distress.

What is the difference between exploration and play?

Exploration and play are so closely linked that researchers are far from unanimous in agreeing about the distinction between the two. Exploration can occur with a familiar toy as the child discovers a new property previously overlooked. Most often, the child alternates between exploration and play. Perhaps the difference between exploration and play is most obvious when observing a child playing with a new toy. First the toy is explored, turned over, tentatively tested. Then play begins.

Exploration applies not only to objects, but to symbols and rules, too. For example, children first learn a word's correct use or meaning, and then play with the word to see what they can do with it.

Little is known about the child's perspective of exploration and play. As A.W. Gottfried (1985a) points out, we do not know whether the child perceives the experiences as separate or whether or not both are intrinsically motivating activities.

Exploration and play appear to be the trial and error process of first finding out what an object or rule is, and then experimenting with what one can do with it. One of the learning values of these dual experiences appears to be children's willingness to engage in and extend the trial and error process whereby they learn rules and then suspend or break them in order to create a product, thought, or solution.

Play is the essence of life

The most important foundation for children's healthy development is the reciprocally pleasurable play between adults and children (Caldwell, 1985). Furthermore, it appears that this playful disposition toward life can carry over from childhood to adulthood. Caldwell summed up the essence of this chapter in her statement that "playful play is related to all things that we want young children to learn to do" (p. 174).

Different Ways
To Look at Play

Play changes with—and therefore reflects—children's development. Many researchers and theorists have attempted to classify these changes by observing children's play at various ages, in a variety of situations, and with children from other cultures. The work of two people seems to have stood the test of time: Piaget (1951/1962) focused primarily on children's play as it relates to their cognitive development, whereas Parten (1932) concentrated on children's social development.

These two systems have been adapted and combined by other researchers in an effort to refine and expand these original groundbreaking taxonomies of play. This chapter will center on these different ways to look at children's play.

How play changes with cognitive and physical development

According to Piaget (1951/1962), children's first 24 months, termed the sensorimotor stage, are dominated by *practice play*. From ages 2 through 7 years, the preoperational stage, children engage mostly in *symbolic play*. Then from ages 7 through 12 and beyond, the concrete operational stage, children are primarily interested in *games with rules*.

Although each type of play may characterize one stage of cognitive and physical development more than others, in this chapter we will refer to the forms of play as *types* rather than stages because there is a great deal of overlap, and children are continually progressing in each type. We must remember that practice play and symbolic play do not drop out with subsequent stages. In fact, any single episode of children's play may reflect more than one type of play. As each new type of play becomes a part of children's repertoire, the other types are retained but may occupy less of the child's time:

> For Tim's first year, he engaged mostly in practice play—picking up and dropping items, crawling, standing, and then walking. At about his first birthday, he began to use symbolic play. He acted as if he were eating or brushing his hair, or pretended to drive a car with his steering wheel. As a toddler, he continued to practice, perfecting new skills such as climbing stairs alone, but much of his play was pretending, floating his boats and cuddling his doll. During the year in which he turned 3, he enjoyed brief games on boards with a dice or spinner to show which color space to move to next—the beginnings of games with rules. He still was practicing, but now learning to pedal his riding toys, and his pretend play grew more sophisticated, with trains built from blocks. By ages 4 and 5, Tim practiced very little; he concentrated mostly on pretending to be a superhero or space character, and enjoyed slightly longer and more complicated games. Once he entered first grade, Tim occasionally engaged in pretend play, and grew very interested in games such as chess and softball.

Even as adults, we continue to practice new skills. Practice play often involves sensorimotor skills at all ages: throwing or reaching, for example. These skills become more complex and are integrated with other motor behaviors as we grow older: skating, biking, or mountain climbing. Some practice may remain at the sensorimotor level to maintain the function or skill, such as with swimming (Gottlieb, 1983). As we learn new strokes, our effort may at first be less playful, but if we practice (assimilate) more than we need to change (accommodate), our effort can be more playful.

Symbolic play also continues beyond the preschool years—as adolescents and adults we daydream, imagining ourselves as a rock star, lottery winner, or bridge expert. Theater productions represent adult versions of symbolic play, albeit in a more formal arrangement!

Games with rules are enjoyed throughout life. Some games involve practice of motor skills or rules (gymnastics, archery), and games generally involve symbols (flags for racing, numbers and letters on playing cards).

Now that we have a sense of just how practice play, symbolic play, and games with rules permeate our entire lives, let us look more closely at how these types of play are evidenced in the lives of young children.

Children who have mastered the alphabet may want to sing the alphabet song repeatedly. Such activities are playful and pleasurable only as long as the level of challenge is under the child's control.

Practice play   Practice activities are divided into three
types by Piaget (1951/1962), with each type
representing varying degrees of foresight
and integration: *mere practice, fortuitous*
combinations, and *intentional combinations.* He also made it clear that
practice play occurs in both the sensorimotor and mental domains.

Mere practice. This type of play involves the practice of some
useful behavior out of its usual context. Although this type of play
predominates in the first 18 months—infants reach, grasp, hit, pat, and
bang objects—older children and even adults engage in mere practice
on occasion. In all cases, mere practice play involves the pleasurable
repetition of skills that have already been mastered: skipping pebbles,
tying and untying shoes, riding a bike.

This type of practice is required to maintain the function (Gottlieb,
1983). No accommodation is required, and thus, in Piaget's terminol-
ogy, the condition of play exists. If other conditions of play are met
(internal motivation, freedom from external rules, attention to means
rather than goal), practice can indeed be called play.

If mere practice comes under external control or violates other
criteria of play, the player is probably less playful (Smith & Vollstedt,
1985). For example, when Lori is forced (externally motivated) to
practice piano, she isn't very playful.

Practice isn't necessarily limited to sensorimotor activities, according to Piaget. *Mental practice,* such as question asking, is yet another
type of practice play. Parents and teachers of preschoolers are familiar
with the children's frequent asking "Why?" "Why?" "Why?" The
focus is not so much to find an answer, but to practice the question-
asking behavior, which makes it *mere practice.*

Memory games and rehearsing easy arithmetic problems *might* constitute mental practice. Children who have mastered the alphabet may
want to sing the alphabet song repeatedly. Such activities are playful
and pleasurable only as long as the level of challenge is under the
child's control (Csikszentmihalyi, 1975). Thus adult-directed drill,
worksheets, flashcards, and other similar so-called teaching techniques
are not play—they are not under the control of the learner.

Fortuitous combinations. A second type of practice play defined by
Piaget is fortuitous combinations: The child uses old schemas with new
combinations that are discovered by accident during mere practice.

> Two-year-old Teresa is rolling and punching her dough clay. Unintentionally, she makes a shape that looks like a hot dog. She smiles at her teacher, points to the clay, and labels it "hot dog."

Fortuitous combinations are reflected in children's stories or other mental schemata created by change in a playful setting. The child might just be thinking of rhyming words, when a new word comes up. Children love to practice small number addition just for fun, while riding in the car for example. In doing so, a child might accidentally discover that $6 + 2$ is the same as $2 + 6$. Fortuitous combinations can be fun!

Older children also encounter fortuitous combinations.

> Seven-year-old Sarah wanted to learn to embroider. She had never done it before, so her grandmother gave her the materials to help her get started. Sarah first got a threaded needle in and out of the fabric. Soon a pattern, wholly unplanned, resulted. She looked at the pattern, labeled the parts, and then created a story: "It's a church. There's a cross, a bowl, and a dipper and they're going to feed the poor."

Intentional combinations. The third and most complex type of practice play involves intentional combinations. Actions, words, or materials may be anticipated and intentionally combined.

> Three-year-old Alicia is playing with small plastic building blocks. She stacks one atop the other, announcing as she goes that she is building a chimney.

Children may use blocks; dough clay; paper with crayons, markers, or paste; wood with hammer and nails—an infinite combination of materials readily available in any good early childhood program—to create bridges, designs, tunnels, or any other item. This play involves using skills already learned by the child to plan and construct. Play that involves anticipatory combinations corresponds to another category called constructive play, identified by Smilansky (1968) and discussed later in this chapter.

Mental practice play may also result in intentional combinations— stories with a variety of interesting words, numbers that all add up to 10 $(9 + 1, 8 + 2, 7 + 3)$. This level of mental practice is only possible after children have mastered the use of words or simple addition.

Children's humor is an excellent example of intentional combinations. At about the age of 5, children catch on to knock-knock jokes. At first, they may imitate older children by merely practicing the question/answer pattern, and may not understand the double meaning of words. A favorite joke of 7-year-olds is:

> *Joshua*: Knock, knock.
> *Virat*: Who's there?
> *Joshua*: Boo.
> *Virat*: Boo who?
> *Joshua*: Oh, you poor dear, why are you crying?

A 5-year-old might tell the joke this way:

> *Lisa*: Knock, knock.
> *Virat*: Who's there?
> *Lisa*: Lisa.
> *Virat*: Lisa who?
> *Lisa*: Lisa Holloman. Ha, ha, ha, ha.

Lisa is still at a level of imitation. She cannot yet reclassify word meanings (accommodation). This mere practice is probably not funny to older children who have mastered the classification-reclassification. Older children may repeat (mere practice) jokes they hear. Most parents and teachers can verify that! As children play with jokes, they may playfully create some of their own combinations, intentionally or fortuitously. This new challenge is one they choose for themselves, not one that can be imposed by an adult if it is to truly be play.

Symbolic play   The second type of play elaborated upon by Piaget is symbolic play, in which the *signifier* is separated from the *signified*. Symbolic play marks the beginning of representational thought through the use of substitute objects or actions.

As we have seen, the first pretend behaviors emerge during the later stages of the sensorimotor period when children practice their own behaviors rather than that of others. Piaget devised a complex framework of stages to describe symbolic play. Because pretend play is such an integral part of the lives of young children, parents and teachers can benefit from a fuller understanding of this type of play.

Stage I. Ages 2 to 4, when language begins, mark the entry into the preoperational period. Several types of symbolic play emerge during this stage.

Symbolic play marks the beginning of representational thought through the use of substitute objects or actions.

Type IA—Children apply schemata already mastered for themselves to others: baby pretends to feed big sister.

Type IB—Children borrow or imitate schemata from the actions of others: older baby pretends to dial the phone.

Type II—Children identify one object with another or their bodies with other people or things: a toddler pretends to pour from a pitcher to a cup.

Type III—Children make four types of symbolic combinations: simple combinations, compensatory combinations, liquidating combinations, and anticipatory symbolic combinations. These combinations are primarily affective and are described in Chapter 3 when we look at children's play from a developmental perspective.

Stage II. During the years from 4 to 7, dramatic play becomes increasingly more accurate in its imitation of reality. Piaget described this phase as being characterized by three features:

Orderliness—Children place the toy dishes in their proper places on the housekeeping area table.

Exact imitation of reality—As the passengers board the pretend bus, they must surrender their paper tokens.

Collective symbolism with differentiation and complementary adjustment of roles—Children agree who will be father, mother, baby, and doggy when they play house.

During this stage, social interaction is incorporated into the children's pretend play, and thus sociodramatic play begins. More about sociodramatic play appears in Chapter 3.

---

*Interest in games with rules increases
between the ages of 6 and 10.*

Stage III. From approximately the ages of 7 to 12, symbolic play declines and is replaced by an interest in games with rules. The symbolic play that remains is often more rule-governed. Roles are more coordinated and expanded, and even more reality-based. Plays, puppet shows, or other performances may be organized, loosely at first, but with predetermined themes. During this stage, children copy reality more closely in their constructions, handiwork, and drawings.

Games with rules A third kind of play with which we are all familiar is games with rules. Piaget defined this favorite pastime as:

Sensory-motor combinations (races, marbles, ball games, etc.), or intellectual combinations (cards, chess, etc.) in which there is competition between individuals (otherwise rules would be useless) and which are regulated either by a code handed down from earlier generations or by temporary agreement. (Piaget 1951/1962, p. 144)

Games with formal rules are played by fewer than 4% of children during the preoperational period from ages 4 to 7 (Rubin, Maioni, & Hornung, 1976; Rubin, Watson, & Jambor, 1978). These games increase in frequency between ages 6 and 10 (Eifermann, 1971), a time when symbolic and practice play decline. This period roughly corresponds to the concrete operational period of cognitive development. Obviously, interest in games with rules remains through adulthood, although they may occupy less of the adult's time. Perhaps for some life becomes a game to be lived, while others take work more seriously.

How play changes with social development

In a classic study of social participation of children from ages 2 to 5, Parten (1932) identified six increasingly complex types of peer play:

Unoccupied—Children watch others at play but do not enter the play. Unoccupied children may just stand around or move about the area.

Onlooker—Children watch others play, may talk to them or ask questions, and seem to move closer to a group, rather than watching whatever momentarily catches their attention.

Solitary independent play—A child plays alone with objects. Even if the child is within speaking distance of others, the child does not alter her or his play, or interact with the others.

Parallel activity—A child plays with toys like those used by nearby children. The child does not try to influence the other children's activities. "He plays *beside* rather than *with* the other children" (Parten, 1932, p. 250).

Associative play—Common activities occur between children. They may exchange toys and/or follow one another. Although all the children in the group are doing similar activities, specific roles are not defined, and there is no organized goal (such as building something or playing a game with rules).

Cooperative or organized supplementary play—Children cooperate with others to construct something, hold competitions, produce dramas with coordinated roles, or play games with formal rules. Group membership is defined, usually by one or two powerful leaders. This type of social play is described more fully in Chapter 3.

Another framework for categorizing types of children's social play was devised by Smilansky (1968). She adapted Piaget's work, adding constructive play as a level between sensorimotor and symbolic play.

Functional play—This category corresponds to Piaget's idea of mere practice play. At this lowest level of play, children repeat simple muscular movements or utterances. This repetitive action provides practice and allows for exploration.

Constructive play—Play materials (dough clay, blocks, paper) are used to create something that remains even after the child has finished playing.

Piaget (1951/1962) classified constructive play as any type of play that is adapted to reality, so constructive play did not comprise a stage in his framework. He believed that the degree of realism determines whether or not the play is constructive. Using his definitions of play, products are created through fortuituous practice play if the child's goal is merely to practice skills, such as building or cutting. However, if the product is planned, it is an intentional combination. If that combination looks realistic, it is constructive practice play, but not a separate stage.

Smilansky's category of constructive play has been criticized by Smith and Vollstedt (1985) as a misunderstanding of Piaget. They claim that constructive play is neither nonliteral nor dominated by means since its purpose is to create something. However, Smilansky's categories have been used, along with other classification systems, in a great deal of research on children's play, and thus it is important to understand how she interpreted this type of play.

Dramatic play—Smilansky's category corresponds to Piaget's category of symbolic play. In dramatic play, according to Smilansky, the child can be an actor, an observer, and a participant in a common enterprise.

Games with rules—This is the highest level of Smilansky's taxonomy. At this level, children accept prearranged rules and adjust to them by controlling their behavior within the limits. Again, her category matches that of Piaget's for games with rules.

Both Parten's and Smilansky's play categories have been combined by Rubin (1977). He reformed the old classification—solitary, parallel, associative, and cooperative; functional, constructive, dramatic, and games with rules—into even more sharply designated categories; for example, solitary-dramatic, solitary-constructive, parallel-constructive, and cooperative games.

In a later revision of his Play Observation Scale, Rubin (1985b) combined associative and cooperative play to form the single category of *group play*. Rubin's scale has been used to assess simultaneous developmental trends in cognitive and social development. This work forms the basis for our discussion in Chapter 3.

In addition, much of the research based on Rubin's taxonomy has been extremely helpful to parents and teachers of young children. For example, his work shows how certain types of toys promote certain forms of play, while other toys inhibit that level of play. Chapter 5 elaborates on the implications of Rubin's work.

Chapter three

How Play Changes
as Children Develop

*C*hildren develop in an orderly and sequential process. This process is characterized by change from the simple to the complex, from concentrating on the self to interacting with others, and from the concrete to the abstract. Play reflects and affects development. Trends are evident in play just as they are in other areas of children's development. Four trends that seem especially pertinent to play have been identified by Garvey (1977):

Biological maturation. As children's bodies and minds grow physically, children gain new skills and competencies. Accurate throwing follows inaccurate throwing. Experience determines the level of skill developed, but maturation provides the possibility.

Elaboration and complexity. Children's play becomes more complicated with age. Two or more resources may be combined.

Control through plans and ideas. Children manipulate the environment or change reality. They are less dependent upon toys or materials, but can use their imaginations.

Wider experiential base. As children see and experience causal relationships among physical and social events, they can use these ideas for pretend themes. Play usually expands from the common "let's play house" to themes about other topics such as astronauts or hospital.

These developmental trends are evident in both the structure and content of children's play. Let us now look closely at how children's play changes from infancy into the early school years.

What and how children practice

Children begin practicing in infancy as they master new skills. These skills may be physical, cognitive, and/or socioemotional. They may involve the body only (watching one's hands), physical objects (feeding oneself), and/or social items (playing This Little Piggy). Children may practice the skills alone, near others, or in a group. Mere practice, fortuituous combinations, and anticipatory combinations may be included.

At each stage of development, children adapt at first quite seriously through exploration (Hutt, 1976). Then, as they master skills, their practice qualifies as play as defined by Piaget (1951/1962). Children's play with objects—toys—has been the center of much research. You have probably seen an infant pick up an object, perhaps a measuring cup. What happens? The cup is turned over in the hands, the handle or edge is put in the mouth, the cup is banged on the floor. Is this exploration or play? Despite the disagreement of various authorities, we do need to see just how the manipulation of objects works to further children's development.

Changes in children's thinking and motor skills   In looking at children's development through a Piagetian framework, we find that in the first 2 years—the sensorimotor stage —children's play often involves objects or their own bodies. Babies love rattles, balls, and their own toes and fingers. Infants look, listen, feel, smell, and taste, first to explore and then to manipulate objects.

During the preschool and early school years, children develop the ability to classify objects (sorting silverware into the proper slots, for example). They develop an understanding of what Piaget terms conservation, seriation, space relations, and temporal relations. How are these ideas learned? Children observe, explore, practice, and experiment. Through these techniques, which are child-directed and may occur accidentally or intentionally, children discover what happens when things or ideas are combined.

Children observe what happens. Before children manipulate objects, people, or their own bodies they observe what happens to them. The first month of life has been described by Piaget as nonplayful because of the great amount of adaptation required for the infant to survive. However, when you watch babies, you see that they soon use their senses, especially looking and listening, to begin to explore their environments.

Contrary to what was even very recently believed, children do see, hear, taste, smell, and feel from birth. Very young babies even can imitate facial expressions and can get bored. Babies can discriminate patterns at birth (Banks & Salapatek, 1983). They begin to explore visually in the first month (Mauer & Salapatek, 1976), preferring faces (Fantz, 1961), patterns with contrast, and things that move (Atkinson, Braddick, & Moar, 1977).

Recent work on infant development reveals that vision is more important than previously thought (see Harris, 1983). It appears that Piaget underestimated the potential for playful practice of visual and auditory skills during the first months of life. Observation, first used soon after birth, continues to be used to investigate new situations throughout adulthood.

The second level of sensorimotor development emerges between 1 and 4 months of age. *Primary circular reactions* is the term used to describe what these infants do best: watch and practice body actions. They watch their hands. Then they notice their arm motions. They begin to repeat their own sounds. Because they cannot yet reach or grasp very well, they cannot manipulate objects. Even rattles, the favorite baby toy, cannot be held in the hands. Instead, children enjoy looking and listening (McCall, 1974). They enjoy contrasts in brightness and staccato movement (McCall, 1979).

Babies as young as 2 months seem to enjoy items they can control (Watson & Ramey, 1972). One mother, aware of research results like this and knowing what her baby could do, devised a toy just right for her baby. She saved small aluminum pie pans, ran a string through the middle of them, and hung them above the baby's feet. What a delightful time her kicking baby had creating a racket! And thus begins the baby's ability to perceive cause and effect relationships.

Children manipulate objects and ideas At about the age of 4 months, infants can begin to appreciate all those rattles given to them as baby gifts. This is the stage of *secondary circular reactions*, in which children can grasp objects, first to explore, and then to play (Collard, 1979). For the next 4 months, babies concentrate on developing their manipulation skills.

Infants seem to prefer new things (Rubenstein, 1976), so don't be surprised if baby drops one rattle the instant another comes into view.

Observation, first used soon after birth, continues to be used to investigate new situations throughout adulthood.

Babies explore not just with their eyes and hands, but especially with their mouths (Belsky & Most, 1981; Uzgiris, 1976). How they love to chew on anything, not only items called toys—brother's finger, the arm of the chair, the strap of the bicycle seat!

Babies also delight in simply looking at objects (Belsky & Most, 1981; Fenson, Kagan, Kearsley, & Zelazo, 1976). Crib mobiles, in which the baby can see what is above, are excellent in these early months.

After exploring objects, infants may increase the level of stimulation by trying out other behaviors with objects (Hutt, 1976). In the later part of this stage, infants get a bang out of hitting two objects together (Fenson et al., 1976). Give baby the spoon and listen to the rhythm as it hits the highchair tray. Now is the time when a piano can act as a giant rattle—the child bangs away to create music, or at least some thunder and lightning! In their play, infants may bang, wave, or pat objects (Collard, 1979).

Piaget (1951/1962; 1963) described the fourth sensorimotor level as *coordination of secondary schemata*. From 8 to 12 months, infants make significant cognitive advances. They intentionally use skills they acquired earlier (mouthing, looking, hitting) in new situations and in new combinations (Piaget, 1951/1962; Uzgiris & Hunt, 1975). Some of these new behaviors include: transferring objects from one hand to the other, turning objects over, extending objects away, fingering, poking, scratching, pulling, and repeatedly grasping and releasing the object with one hand while holding it with the other (Collard, 1979).

During this period, mouthing seems to decrease (Belsky & Most, 1981; McCall, 1974). Simple manipulation remains the dominant mode of exploration, but now babies begin to relate two objects, such as a spoon and dish (Belsky & Most, 1981; Fenson et al., 1976). Infants appear to be more serious in their explorations. They practice and master new skills. They especially benefit from toys that offer contingent reinforcement—a horn honks when they push the yellow button (McCall, 1974).

As we have noted, the difference between play and exploration is not generally agreed upon. One observer suggested that these behaviors were play rather than exploration: banging; waving; patting; rubbing, pushing, or pulling a toy on a surface; and casting. Regardless, these behaviors are common in the months just before a baby's first birthday.

Another indication of a baby's strides in cognitive development is the often maligned stranger anxiety and its related aspect, object permanence. Out of sight is no longer out of mind. When a familiar toy is hidden under a blanket, baby lifts the blanket to retrieve it. Many babies tend to become fearful of strange adults at about this time but are able to recognize clearly those who are familiar.

Beginning around that momentous first birthday is the period called *tertiary circular reactions*. This period lasts for about 6 months, and according to Piaget (1951/1962; 1963) is characterized by active experimentation in order to see the result. Children experiment to find new ways to achieve goals. They may discover that sticks or strings are useful tools to bring an object closer. They may find that a toy works if they push, pull, turn, punch, or poke it (Uzgiris & Hunt, 1975). Wind-up and pop-up toys and toys with buttons to push, knobs to twirl, and switches to flip are a hit at this age (Fenson et al., 1976). By carefully watching children's play, adults can select toys that offer just the right challenge for the baby (McCall, 1974).

Related to the baby's new sense of object permanence is the popularity of fill and dump play in children between 13 and 24 months (Mann, 1984). These children love to fill a container with objects and then dump them out. A milk carton and some tennis balls can lead to lots of fun.

Children between 12 and 18 months also first begin to exhibit early symbolic play: using objects in socially appropriate ways, separating objects from their names, and imitating others. At this age, children can combine objects in a way intended by the manufacturer—they will put the peg in the hole rather than in the mouth (Belsky & Most, 1981). They relate objects to actions—put the lid on the pot (Fenson et al., 1976).

Social activities are also a big hit: drinking from a cup, wearing a necklace, driving a toy car (Uzgiris & Hunt, 1975). These researchers also found that infants could imitate behaviors in which they could not see themselves (copy a funny face) and could repeat new sounds or words. New evidence shows that infants as young as 14 months can imitate gestures even after a 24-hour delay (Meltzoff, 1985). This finding seems to confirm that symbolic play indeed has its roots in the sensorimotor period (Fein, 1981a; Fein & Apfel, 1979; Fenson & Ramsay, 1980).

The sixth level of sensorimotor development ranges from 18 to 24 months. It is characterized as the *invention of means through mental combinations*—problems may be solved through foresight rather than trial and error. While object manipulation is still more prevalent than pretend play, simple manipulation declines, especially from 18 to 21 months (Belsky & Most, 1981). At the same time, children increasingly can combine objects in socially appropriate ways (Fenson et al., 1976). Thus, these older infants are more interested in fitting objects (nesting blocks within blocks or putting shapes into holes) than in filling and dumping (Mann, 1984; DeLoache, Sugarman, & Brown, 1985).

Practice play continues through the preoperational period from 2 to 7 years. Physical and mental actions continue to be involved. Language play in the preschool years may involve repetitious question-asking ("Why?") or the creation of interesting word/sound patterns and stories. Children this age perfect their basic movement skills: They run, jump, skip, and gallop, and then incorporate these skills in chasing, racing, and aiming games.

During these years, children explore first single objects then relationships between objects (DeLoache et al., 1985). Thus, through practice children try to make something (Rubin, Watson, & Jambor, 1978; Smilansky, 1968). Constructive play seems to be the predominant type of play among middle-class preschoolers (Johnson & Ershler, 1981; Rubin & Maioni, 1975; Smilansky, 1968). These planned combinations are more likely to involve others as children grow older (Rubin, 1985a).

Playful practice with words characterizes the early school years: Antonyms, homonyms, and synonyms evolve into riddles, poems, songs, and chants. At first, riddles may simply be repeated, then combined by accident or foresight to create new ones.

Increased small muscle control in the hand and wrist enables school-aged children to draw, do simple needlework, and build models.

We have seen that children's development enables them to play in ways that are more and more sophisticated. One study confirmed what parents and teachers have learned from experience: When presented with open-ended play materials, 4- and 5-year-olds made simple constructions using few materials; 6- and 7-year-olds made more constructions and used more materials; 8- to 10-year-olds made fewer but more complex constructions and integrated more types of materials (Vandenberg, 1981a).

Similarly, fundamental movement skills from the preschool and kindergarten period are combined by the young school-aged child into complex motor tasks such as cartwheels and backward rolls. Children may practice them alone or near others, sometimes in combination with social rules, and thus games with rules emerge. As children master each new skill, they look for ways to increase the challenge. Jump rope is altered to become double-dutch jump rope. When they have mastered diving from the low diving board, many children move to the high board without need for encouragement from others.

Changes in children's social interaction

Adult/child play
Two people are usually involved in early adult/child play: the baby and a parent or caregiver; other people or objects are excluded from attention (Bakeman & Adamson, 1984). What happens in these interactions? The baby and adult look intently at each other (mutual gazing) and exchange synchronized sounds and smiles much as in a conversation (Bakeman & Brown, 1977).

As we have seen, young infants are interested in visually exploring objects even before they can manipulate them. Some evidence indicates that babies may focus on either people or objects, but not both simultaneously, and that between 6 and 18 months they spend more time playing with objects than people (Bakeman & Adamson, 1984). During this time, parents and caregivers support object play by manipulating objects (shaking the rattle, tossing the ball) to capture the infant's attention. This has been called *passive joint engagement*—both the adult and infant focus on the toy and neither seems aware of the other's actions. Gradually infants begin to coordinate their attention into coordinated joint play (Bakeman & Adamson, 1984). The structure of adult/child play clearly parallels developments in the child's capabilities.

At each new level of development the adult supports the infant's development by eliciting the most complex skills of which the infant is capable. In a study of parents of 7-, 10-, and 13-month-olds, parents of the oldest infants were more likely to encourage pretend play, turn taking, and social relations. They were less likely to direct the baby's attention or to perform for their babies (Power, 1985).

This technique of performing attention-getting actions and setting the stage for appropriate responses has been called *scaffolding* (Bruner & Sherwood, 1976). Let's look at some of the research that supports the idea of scaffolding.

In roll-the-ball games, mothers held out their hands to set the stage for the baby to reciprocate by returning the ball (Hodapp, Goldfield, & Boyatzis, 1984). In their early versions of Peek-a-Boo, mothers covered themselves and then leaned forward and made sounds to get their babies to watch or even to remove the cover (Hodapp et al., 1984).

When behaviors like these are used, babies are most successful at the game. Nevertheless, children's interest plays a large part (Power & Parke, 1983). The chances for infant success are higher when parents interfere less—when the adult focuses on the object and does not attempt to change the object of play (Power, 1985).

Children can learn and practice social rules through adult/infant play (Bruner & Sherwood, 1976). Some of these rules of social interaction include

- mutual involvement,
- role repetition,
- turn taking, and
- nonliterality (Ross & Kay, 1980).

Think for a minute about the game Pat-a-Cake. The players are mutually involved, focusing their eyes on each other and then on their hands. Actions are repeated in turns. The adult may pat the cakes and then pause, as if to say, "It's your turn." The baby's role may be to smile or laugh at her or his turn (role repetition). Then the baby pauses to let the adult do it again. The play is nonliteral because there are no real cakes.

During the preschool years, children are increasingly involved in social interactions with same-age friends.

During the preschool years, children are increasingly involved in social interaction with same-age friends (Barnes, 1971; Parten, 1932; Smith, 1978). Even so, adult/child interactional play continues (Harper & Huie, 1985). Some of this play involves body maneuvers, facial expressions, and play with language. A fun game might involve a ritual of taking motor skills out of their usual context. Games and rituals from infancy become more sophisticated: Gonna-Get-You becomes chase; Peek-a-Boo becomes Hide-and-Seek; Pat-a-Cake becomes a complex game of Pease Porridge Hot.

At the same time, rituals may be invented by accident (fortuitous combination) or, later, by plan (anticipatory combination).

One day Mom was listening to Dad and ignoring 4-year-old Jenny. Jenny attempted to get attention by holding her mother's chin and pulling Mom's face closer to her own. Mom continued to listen to Dad but kept her face contorted with her chin pushed aside. When Dad finished, Mom turned her eyes to Jenny and said in a funny voice, "Look, you made my face crooked." Jenny pushed Mom's chin back the other way, but pushed it too far. Mom said, almost laughing and with a glint in her eye, "Look, now it's crooked on the other side." Jenny pulled the chin back the other way, careful to stop in the middle. Mom said, "Now it's crooked in the middle." This resulted in roars of laughter and was repeated at Jenny's request for five rounds.

This ritual, begun by accident, was repeated periodically into Jenny's early school years. The episode contains all the elements necessary for playful social interaction: It involved turns, mutual interaction, role repetition, and nonliterality. It was dominated by the child's action and occurred without threat in a playful manner. This ritual was used to renew the closeness of Jenny and Mom's relationship, akin to Erikson's (1977) concept of the ritual of recognition which helps maintain trust and possibly attachment.

The school years bring another increase in peer play accompanied by a decrease in the proportion of time children spend playing with adults. Even so, parents, teachers, and recreation leaders may participate as children swim, dance, or joke around playfully.

Adults also introduce more complex strategy games such as checkers or Monopoly™. Usually children explore the game in a few sessions before they actually practice it while adhering to the rules. This gradual acquisition is done with little competition, rules are loosely applied, and rules may not fully be understood, which is why learning these games is included with practice play.

Teaching young children games may be much like the scaffolding role in adult/infant games (Bruner & Sherwood, 1976). The adult may guarantee success by supporting the child's attempts, even pointing out to the child moves that will ultimately lead to the adult's defeat (purchase a property whenever you land on it). This early adult/child practice is a steppingstone to cooperative games with rules that children enforce more stringently when playing with peers.

Peer play   Most children's play progresses from solitary behavior to social cooperation (Barnes, 1971; Parten, 1932; Smith, 1978). The first child/child interactions often occur near the middle of the first year when infants make sounds or smile to or touch each other. This is called *patterned interaction* (Eckerman & Whatley, 1977; Hay, Nash, & Pedersen, 1983; Jacobson, 1981; Vandell, Wilson, & Buchanan, 1980). These first interactions are usually brief and do not involve toys (Hay et al., 1983; Jacobson, 1981; Vandell et al., 1980). However, toward the end of the first year toys may be included (Jacobson, 1981; Vandell et al., 1980).

In the second year of life, peer interactions are more frequent and coordinated (Eckerman & Whatley, 1977; Mueller & Brenner, 1977). They also last longer and are more likely to involve objects (Mueller & Brenner, 1977). Infants in the second year of life bring to social situations the abilities to

• repeat their own behavior,
• understand and imitate their partner's behavior,
• get their partner's attention, and
• create interaction by making their behaviors interesting (Hay, Ross, & Goldman, 1979).

Taking turns may be done through simple imitation, and may occur for several rounds. Older toddlers reciprocate actions rather than imitate them (Mueller & Lucas, 1975). Games such as ball roller/ball catcher and chaser/chased are popular. Verbal exchanges may be of the "No, I'm not"/"You are too" type (Garvey, 1979).

More interactions and coordination of social play are evidenced as children mature. Unoccupied, solitary, and parallel play decline during the preschool years, while associative and cooperative play increase as children approach kindergarten (Parten, 1932). Similar trends have been found in recent research using several cultural groups (Barnes, 1971; Harper & Huie, 1985; Rubin, 1977; Rubin & Maioni, 1975; Rubin, Maioni, & Hornung, 1976) and longitudinal data (Johnson & Ershler, 1981; Smith, 1978).

Several researchers are now questioning whether Parten's levels actually constitute a continuum, however, and have proposed alternate views of solitary and parallel play instead. Solitary play is often comprised of goal-directed, educational, or large motor play, and thus cannot be said to represent social withdrawal or immaturity (Johnson & Ershler, 1981; Moore, Evertson, & Brophy, 1974; Rubin et al., 1976).

Solitary play may indicate that preschool children are choosing to "get away from it all" (Rubin et al., 1976, p. 418), whereas those who play beside others may wish to interact but lack the skills to play in an associative or cooperative manner.

Parallel play, not solitary play, has been proposed as the least mature form of social participation by Rubin et al. (1976) and Johnson, Ershler, and Bell (1980). Still others have proposed that parallel play and solitary play represent separate dimensions, rather than points on a continuum (Roper & Hinde, 1978), and that how much a child plays alone is not related to how much the child interacts when playing with others.

Perhaps the function and use of parallel play changes with developmental level. Parallel play may serve as an intermediate level between solitary and group play for some 2-year-olds, but not for 3- and 4-year-olds who move mainly from solitary to group behavior (Smith, 1978). Therefore, Smith concludes that parallel play might not reflect greater social maturity than solitary play. Solitary play may be an option for older preschoolers, whereas younger ones who lack skills for making friends may have little choice but to play alone unless a sensitive adult can help them gain entry to a group.

Another perspective views parallel play as a short-term strategic bridge toward more social involvement, rather than as a developmental stage (Bakeman & Brownlee, 1980). These researchers propose that parallel play occurs for a matter of minutes, during which time the players size up nearby children and begin to coordinate actions.

Indeed, parallel play seems to facilitate interaction among unfamiliar toddlers (Mueller & Brenner, 1977). Parallel play, such as tagging along, may serve as a strategy to gain social acceptance, especially for young and/or inexperienced preschoolers, whereas it would be less useful for experienced and acquainted 4-year-olds.

Children's social participation can also be linked to their cognitive development (Johnson & Ershler, 1981). The Play Observation Scale referred to earlier (Rubin, 1977, 1985b; Rubin & Maioni, 1975; Rubin et al., 1976) combines the social play categories listed by Parten (1932) with the cognitive categories identified by Smilansky (1968). Using this scale, it appears that with increasing age from preschool to kindergarten there is a decrease in solitary-functional, solitary-dramatic, and parallel-functional play, while there is an increase in parallel-constructive play and group dramatic play (Rubin, 1982b; Rubin, Watson, & Jambor, 1978).

Other results of studies that combined social and cognitive categories have also shed light on the issue of maturity verses solitary and parallel play. In essence, the developmental outcome of various levels of social interaction depends on the level of cognitive play with which it is combined.

In one study, 4-year-old children who engaged in more solitary play than their peers were judged as having low social competence if their play was at the functional level (Smilansky's lowest category). However, those who were solitary players at the constructive level were not judged as low in social competence (Rubin, 1982b). Parallel-functional play seemed to be a transitional sensorimotor type of behavior that brought children into conflict. However, parallel-constructive play was associated positively with mental age, sociometric ratings, social problem-solving skills, and complexity of play constructions. Parallel-dramatic play decreased with age, presumably as children increased in their role-taking ability (Rubin, 1982b).

Changes in children's symbolic play

Sometime around children's first birthdays, they begin to use actions and words to convey nonliteral meanings—they pretend to feed their stuffed animals or talk on the telephone. Representational activities like these are the essence of symbolic play. Pretend play continues to increase throughout the preschool years. Children's symbolic play gradually involves more abstract and preplanned representations, and their play with adults and peers changes as well. As we saw earlier in this book, symbolic play continues throughout life in the form of fantasy and formal dramas.

Children's fantasy play is often called sociodramatic play—make-believe (dramatic play) that involves social interactions. Before these planned sequences of social role enactments can occur, however, children must mature considerably, both socially and cognitively.

It appears that at least two social resources are needed for dramatic play:

• *knowledge* of the social world: people's roles, relationships between people, and how people carry out roles and maintain relationships, and
• *ability to communicate with social partners* to negotiate roles, settings, and action sequences (Garvey, 1977).

In the process of developing these resources, three cognitive trends in symbolic play are evidenced in young children (Fenson, 1985):

• *decentration*—the "increasing tendency to incorporate other participants in pretend activities" (Fenson, 1985, p. 34). This shift from a focus on oneself to others begins around the age of 18 months (Fein, 1975).
• *decontextualization*—the increasing ability to transform objects and actions in order to symbolically represent other objects or actions. Between the ages of about 20 and 26 months, children become less dependent on realistic props (Fein, 1975). Thus, children move from

concrete to abstract symbols and can increasingly separate the signifier from the signified.

• *integration*—the increasing ability to combine more than one object or action sequence to portray more complex events and sequences. Children's play increases in complexity both in the number of schemes used (Nicolich, 1977) and in the number of transformations, such as object substitutions (Fein, 1975).

Early indicators of these trends were first described by Piaget (1951/ 1962) and later mapped out by Nicolich (1977) (see Table). Bretherton (1984) then summarized these sequential developments according to the changes children undergo in roles, actions, and objects.

Roles become more complex

Children represent themselves. Children's first pretend behaviors usually are practice of their own activities out of their usual context—the actions are self-referenced. Children may practice eating, sleeping, or hand washing in a nonrealistic setting (they are not really hungry, sleepy, or dirty). This behavior has been referred to as the *autosymbolic* scheme (Nicolich, 1977).

Although Piaget (1951/1962) realized that early pretense involved symbolic practice, he noted that the behaviors were not symbols of the behavior of others, but of the child's own schemata. Therefore, he did not include self-representation as a type of symbolic play.

Children act on others. After children have practiced imitating their own actions, they begin to apply them, one at a time, to other people or objects. Children begin to tuck their dolls into bed. They may offer their toy horse a bit of cereal. Washing dolls is great fun! Children use what is familiar in their daily pattern of life, and apply it to others (Fein, 1975; Watson & Fischer, 1977). However, children do not yet simultaneously portray the feelings, thoughts, or actions of the recipient.

Among the trends that have been noted are an increase in feeding dolls and a decrease in feeding self between the ages of 12 and 30 months (Fein & Apfel, 1979). These researchers also found that during this same age span, children used another person, such as mother, less often as a recipient of the action.

Piaget called children's application of behaviors from their own experience to others *projection of symbolic schemes onto new objects.* Nicolich included it in the first stage of symbolic play (see Table).

Sequence of Symbolic Levels According to Piaget and as Applied in this Research

Piaget (1962)	Nicolich Levels and Criteria	Examples
Sensorimotor Period Prior to Stage VI	(1) Presymbolic Scheme: The child shows understanding of object use or meaning by brief recognitory gestures.	The child picks up a comb, touches it to his hair, drops it.
	No pretending.	The child picks up the telephone receiver, puts it into ritual conversation position, sets it aside.
	Properties of present object are the Stimulus.	
	Child appears serious rather than playful.	The child gives the mop a swish on the floor.
Stage VI	(2) Auto-symbolic Scheme: The child pretends at self-related activities. Pretending.	The child simulates drinking from a toy baby bottle.
	Symbolism is directly involved with the child's body.	The child eats from an empty spoon.
	Child appears playful, seems aware of pretending.	The child closes his eyes, pretending to sleep.
Symbolic Stage I	(3) Single Scheme Symbolic Games Child extends symbolism beyond his own actions by:	
Type I A Assimilative	A. Including other actors or receivers of action, such as doll or mother.	Child feeds mother or doll (A). Child grooms mother or doll (A).
Type I B Imitative	B. Pretending at activities of other people or objects such as dogs, trucks, trains, etc.	Child pretends to read a book (B). Child pretends to mop floor (B). Child moves a block or toy car with appropriate sounds of vehicle (B)
These distinctions are not made by Piaget	(4) Combinatorial Symbolic Games 4.1 Single Scheme Combinations: One pretend scheme is related to several actors or receivers of action.	Child combs own, then mother's hair. Child drinks from the bottle, feeds doll from bottle. (4.1) Child puts an empty cup to mother's mouth, then experimenter, and self. (4.1)
	4.2 Multi-scheme Combinations: Several schemes are related to one another in sequence.	Child holds phone to ear, dials. Child kisses doll, puts it to bed, puts spoon to its mouth. (4.2) Child stirs in the pot, feeds doll, pours food into dish. (4.2)
	(5)Planned Symbolic Games: Child indicates verbally or non-verbally that pretend acts are planned before being executed.	Child finds the iron, sets it down, searches for the cloth, tossing aside several objects. When cloth is found, she irons it. (5.1)
	5.1 Planned Single Scheme Symbolic Acts Transitional Type: Activities from levels 2–3 that are planned.	Child picks up play screw-driver, says "toothbrush" and makes the motions of toothbrushing. (5.1)
Type II A	Type A Symbolic identification of one object with another.	
Type II B	Type B Symbolic identification of the child's body with some other person or object.	Child picks up the bottle, says "baby," then feeds the doll and covers it with a cloth. (5.2)
Type III A	5.2 Combinations With Planned Elements: These are constructed of activities from Levels 2–5.1, but always include some planned element. They tend toward realistic scenes.	Child puts play foods in a pot, stirs them. Then says "soup" or "Mommy" before feeding the mother. She waits, then says "more?" offering the spoon to the mother. (5.2)

Nicolich, L. M. (1977). Beyond sensorimotor intelligence: Assessment of symbolic maturity through analysis of pretend play. *Merrill-Palmer Quarterly, 23*, 89–99. Reprinted by permission of the Wayne State University Press.

Children represent another's behavior. Symbolic play begins, according to Piaget, when children begin to apply their own behaviors (feeding) to another recipient (feeding mother) or to apply another's behavior (father shaving) to themselves. These behaviors were called imitation by Piaget, and comprise Level 3, Type B on Nicolich's scale (see Table).

Children's play of this type happens after the child has observed the behavior, so it is called *deferred imitation.*

> Marta pretends to read the newspaper, imitating her parent's behaviors by turning the pages and moving her head from side to side. Similarly, she pretends to cook by pouring into a bowl and stirring vigorously.

These early beginnings of role play, in which children enact the behavior of another person (Bretherton, 1984), have been observed as early as 14 months (Meltzoff, 1985).

Before children can engage in sociodramatic play, they must mature considerably, both socially and cognitively.

Children take on parallel roles. Later in toddler development, children may begin to act upon more than one recipient. David may "comb" his own hair, and then comb Daddy's hair. Toddlers enjoy this "first me, then you" sequence of events. When children incorporate both themselves and then others into a pretend sequence of a single scheme (hair combing), they exhibit a more complex level of symbolism (Bretherton, 1984).

Children use replicas as active recipients. When children first use dolls or other realistic looking objects, these replicas are passive recipients of the child's action. However, when children treat them as if they can feel or act, the recipient is referred to as active (Bretherton, 1984; Fenson, 1984).

> Christine sits her bear in the highchair, saying, "There you go." She then offers a spoon with "honey," asking her bear, "You like honey, don't you?"

By talking to her bear, Christine implies that bears can hear and have preferences, something passive recipients would not.

Others have labeled these pretend behaviors in a different way. Watson and Fischer (1977) called dolls and other substitutes *passive recipients* even when children ascribed perceptual traits to them. These theorists used *active agent* to describe when the child acted out behaviors of the agent.

Children use replicas as agents. In a slightly higher level of representation, the replica, such as a doll or toy horse, is active (Watson & Fischer, 1977). Dolls may walk, or talk, or cry. Unlike Christine's active recipient bear, who seemed to have feelings but did not act, at this level the bear would be an agent, and Christine would talk for it, saying "Yummy, I like honey!"

Children assume another person's role. This level of pretend play is familiar to parents and early childhood educators:

Tyisha becomes a doctor, no longer just giving an injection because she is copying that behavior, but giving it because she is the doctor and that is part of the many duties for the role of doctor.

Jae Me is the bus driver. Passengers are asked to move back after handing over their tickets. Stops are announced, and the brakes screech as the bus slows.

When children enact roles, or play games of imitation in Piagetian terms, their bodies are identified with or used to symbolize another's body or thing. The first roles are usually the most familiar ones, such as mommy or daddy (Garvey, 1977). Later, children may play roles they may not have experienced or interacted with:

Ryan is a cowboy. He gallops along on his stick horse yelling "Gidday up!" and "Whoa!"

Denise is a watch dog. She hides behind a cabinet, then pounces out to scare her teacher, barking "Woof! Woof!"

Sebastian is a train. "Here comes the train," he announces. "Whooo, whooo! Watch out or I will run over you!"

Children can pretend to be other people, animals, or even things. They begin with a single scheme, and imitate increasingly complex behaviors and characteristics. Nicolich (1977) includes this symbolic identification with another person or object at the level of planned symbolic acts.

Children use dolls as active partners. As children become more aware of and sensitive to others, they are able to understand another's role and keep it in mind while at the same time carrying out their own role (Fenson & Ramsay, 1980). How much more cognitively sophisticated this play is!

At this level, children first make it possible for the replica to act; they may place a bottle in the babydoll's hand (Fenson & Ramsay, 1980). Then, when reciprocal action with the doll begins, the child must enact two roles: self and doll. Perhaps the child will act as a mother for the doll, and will also act by speaking and acting for the doll itself (Miller & Garvey, 1984).

Behaviors such as these are classified at a higher level than that of just the doll acting because one other reciprocal role is involved (Bretherton, 1984).

Children engage in simple collaborative role play. How much more difficult it becomes when children act out roles in collaboration with another person! They must adjust their script in accordance with the wishes of their partner. Practice, experience, and an increased ability to understand another's perspective contribute as children gradually become successful collaborators.

This type of play seems to be facilitated and become more elaborate when the partner is more mature and experienced (an older child, parent, or caregiver, for example) (Bretherton, 1984). This partner can ask questions, introduce props, or in other noninterfering ways suggest what action might happen next.

> Three-year-old Jorge is in his playroom pushing his fire truck around. Alberto, his 5-year-old brother, joins him on the floor with an ambulance. "Quick, there is a fire down the street," Alberto cries. Jorge's fire truck and Alberto's ambulance rush to the scene. "Water, we need water to put out the fire," Jorge yells. "Here's some water," offers Alberto. "Now we need to rescue the people."

Children use replicas with several interacting roles. Dolls, tigers, astronauts, and mail carriers are just some of the many replicas children find fascinating. At this level, children may combine several replicas, talking both about and for each of them. With this increasing complexity in role differentiation comes the ability to play more than one role simultaneously, such as husband and father (Bretherton, 1984). This type of pretend play is categorized by Nicolich (1977) as a combination of planned elements comprised of multiple role enactments.

Children play collaboratively with several roles. If children are to successfully play with others, they must refine and integrate their role-taking skills. Complex dramas of this type are often observed in children ages 3 and 4, who enjoy playing family or enacting events such as birthday parties. These dramas involve planning to coordinate the multiple combinations of roles and object substitutions (Nicolich, 1977). Each child brings to the scene her or his own concepts of familiar events and actions, and these ideas form the basis for communicating and planning (Nelson & Seidman, 1984).

Three types of social roles are often enacted, according to Garvey (1977):

• *functional roles*—some job or action must be done. Drivers drive. Cooks cook.

• *character roles*—either stereotyped or fictional, they may symbolize an "occupation, habitual action, habitual attitude, or personality feature" (p. 89). Stereotyped roles include witches or monsters. Occupations commonly portrayed include teacher, pilot, and doctor. Fictional characters—Wonder Woman, ALF, or Cookie Monster—are popular.

• *family roles*—mother, father, baby, sister, and brother are common in preschool dramatic play.

Themes change as children mature. At age 3, children focus on adorning the body, meal preparation, feeding, bedtime routine, and travel (Forys & McCune-Nicolich, 1984). Younger children tend to enact roles they have experienced (baby) or that are reciprocal to their own experience (mother or father), while older preschoolers are able to enact roles they have observed but not experienced or reciprocated (husband and wife) (Garvey, 1977).

Actions range from single schemes to complex sequences

Children begin with single schemes. Before children can pretend, they must have some concept about what is real. Before they can represent an action, object, or role out of context, they must understand it in context. Therefore, Nicolich (1977) includes a presymbolic scheme level in which the child shows an understanding of a real object by demonstrating the proper way to use it. For example, baby may swipe at the kitchen counter with a dish cloth.

However, it is often difficult to tell whether the child is merely using the object appropriately, or whether the child is pretending (Bretherton, 1984). Is Beth trying to get a real drink from an empty cup (showing that she knows what to do with a cup), or is she pretending? Careful observation may reveal the answer. If Beth is thirsty and appears to be emotionally stressed, she is probably not pretending.

Children combine schemes. Sometime around the end of a baby's first year, single schemes are occasionally combined (Nicolich, 1977).

• A single scheme may be applied to several recipients. Wendy kisses her bear, her rabbit, and her sheep (parallel roles).

• Different schemes can be carried out in succession. Wendy kisses her bear and then feeds it.

Unrelated scheme combinations are observed infrequently (Nicolich, 1977) but are used by most children by the age of 19 months (Fenson & Ramsay, 1980, 1981). This low frequency may be because most combinations that children use are related and thus belong to the next higher level (Bretherton, 1984).

Children order several schemes. When children combine different schemes and carry them out in a logical order, their activity is called *ordered multischemes* (Bretherton, 1984; Fenson & Ramsay, 1980, 1981). For example, a child may pretend to fill a cup and then offer a drink to his doll. The number of multischemes increases between 19 and 24 months (Fenson & Ramsay, 1980), and grows from just two schemes to four or more sequenced acts (Bretherton, 1984): A child may fill a cup, feed his doll, and then burp it.

Children combine episodes. Once children can combine schemes, they can organize them into longer episodes that resemble dramas. After feeding and burping the doll (feeding episode) the child may put the doll to bed, cover it and then tell it to go to sleep (bedtime episode).

Objects represent real and then imaginary items

Children use objects as substitutes. Using an object, perhaps a block, to represent a train, for example, is known as *object substitution*. Piaget (1951/1962) called object substitution the simple identification of one object for another.

When children first begin to substitute objects, at about the age of 14 months, the object and what it represents must be fairly similar. This type of play becomes more frequent between 19 and 24 months, when children enjoy small replicas of cups, plates, cars, airplanes, and people (Fein, 1981a). Later, less prototypical toys are needed (Fein, 1981a; Fein & Apfel, 1979; Watson & Fischer, 1977). In fact, less realistic toys promote more diverse play themes among 4- to 8-year-olds (Pulaski, 1970).

The number of simultaneous substitutions that children can make increases with development (Fein, 1975). In Fein's study, 90% of the 24-month-old children could pretend to feed a horse when both horse and feed were realistic. Only 70% could handle one substitution, and just 33% were able to pretend when neither horse nor feed was realistic.

The nature of the substitute objects may also influence children's ability to make transformations. It is easier to substitute an ambiguous object, such as a block, than it is to substitute a highly realistic one that suggests another use (Fein, 1981a). For example, children are more likely to comb their hair with a block than with a car.

Children mime. Symbolizing roles, actions, or objects without using physical props is called miming. Children invent imaginary objects, and can do so when requested at least as early as 30 months (Elder & Pederson, 1978; Overton & Jackson, 1973). Children as young as 23 months, but not as young as 16 months, could imitate a model's inventions (Jackowitz & Watson, 1980).

There are definitely developmental differences in the nature of children's creations (Overton & Jackson, 1973). When 3- to 8-year-olds were asked to pretend without an object for a prop, younger ones used a body part such as a finger for a toothbrush, a form of object substitution. Older children imagined they were holding the toothbrush.

Indeed, there may be two levels of invention—with and without physical supports (Ungerer, Zelazo, Kearsley, & O'Leary, 1981). At first, children imagine an object when another physical reminder is present.

> Norm is baking imaginary cookies. He uses a bowl and spoon (physical props) to stir the batter. He comments, "Oh my, this dough is too thick to stir."

Later, children are able to invent without physical props. Fenson (1984) observed children as young as 31 months miming, while Ungerer et al. (1981) found the youngest age to be 34 months. A number of differences in the studies, or between the children involved, could account for this age range.

Imaginary playmates are also invented substitutes. However, they do not offer an opportunity for interaction that can contribute to children's growing social skills (Rosen, 1974). Reciprocal role play requires that the child assume the role of another, and that a peer can cooperate and communicate to plan the play.

How children communicate about their symbolic play

Before children can play with others, they must be able to communicate. Their interactions are characterized by mutual involvement, role repetition, and turn taking (Ross & Kay, 1980). In infancy, children first learn to communicate with the important adults in their lives. As they interact with peers, these skills are modified. With each year, children use longer sentences, bigger words, and more complex ideas.

Ritual plays a key part in the development of communication. Most rituals are based on controlled repetitions with a steady rhythm. See if you can detect the qualities of ritual in this example of four 3-year-olds seated at the table for lunch.

> *Ben:* "This spaghetti looks like worms."
> *Margot:* "This spaghetti looks like squirms."
> *Adam:* "This spaghetti looks like germs."
> *Jessica:* "This spaghetti looks like derms."
> *Adam:* "This spaghetti looks like goo goo."
> *Margot:* "This spaghetti looks like candy bars."
> *Adam:* "Hey, here comes dessert."

Language was clearly the basic resource in this ritual, but social exchanges are also involved. Rituals can also involve physical actions. These social exchanges have a rhythm—even pauses between speakers may count as part of the beat.

With age, children are increasingly able to pretend and communicate. They may negotiate roles and plans for action, first practicing negotiation through ritual.

> Two 5-year-olds are sitting in the back seat on a long car trip. For nearly 60 minutes, they negotiate, never carrying out any action. First they negotiate roles.

> *Sarah:* "Let's pretend we're lions."
> *Rachel:* "No, no. Let's pretend we're tigers."
> *Sarah:* "I know. Let's pretend we're elephants."
> *Rachel:* "Let's pretend we're (names another role)."
> *Sarah:* "Let's pretend we're (names another role)."

> After numerous repetitions, they change from negotiating roles to negotiating settings.

> *Sarah:* "Let's pretend we're at the circus."
> *Rachel:* "Let's pretend we're at the beach."
> *Sarah:* "I know. Let's pretend we're on the moon."
> *Rachel:* "Yeah, yeah. Let's pretend we're on spaceships."
> *Sarah:* "Let's pretend we're (names setting)."

Rachel: "Wow. Let's pretend we're (names setting)."

This play continues for 30 minutes.

Apparently children who learn turn-taking rituals as infants adopt these schemes with peers. They may practice the negotiation ritual without ever going into enough detail to extend the play through action. Mature children who know each other well might set a complex pretend play sequence into action with a simple cue such as: "Let's play. . . ."

The ways in which children give messages to each other that "this is play" are fascinating (Bateson, 1956). Children understand that they are playing, but also that their play stands for reality (and more). Two types of metacommunication are involved. *Out-of-frame* communications are not part of the play script, but are messages or rules about the play: "No dogs are allowed in this house." *Within-frame* communications are the dialogue of the play itself.

What techniques do children use as they talk during their play? Giffin (1984) has identified several, based on observations of children from ages 3 to 7:

• *play enactment*—the least mature level, when play evolves without discussion.

• *ulterior conversation*—indirect statements in the play script that hint at a change in the text: "I wish Mom would get home from work."

• *underscoring*—comments that define actions or states while in acting them out: "I'm feeding the baby."

• *storytelling*—narration, in a singsong cadence, while acting: "And then I baked some cookies." With this method, the child can elicit the next behavior in the sequence without formal negotiation with other players.

• *prompting*—moving out of the play frame briefly to clarify text or to direct others. The child abandons the voice and posture associated with the role, may use a low voice, and gives brief directions: "Now pretend you're the teacher," "You're supposed to say the blessing."

• *implicit pretend structuring*—"negotiations that overtly establish the major elements of the action plan, but still do not verbally acknowledge the pretense" (Giffin, 1984, p. 86). "It's time for us to go to the store."

• *overt proposals to pretend*—extended out-of-frame behavior or metacommunication. "Let's pretend this is a hospital and I will be the doctor. Here is my office, and there is where the patients wait."

Before children can coordinate pretend play, they must share some common knowledge of the script (Nelson & Seidman, 1984). Therefore grocery shopping, birthday parties, and other familiar events are popular because the sequence, setting, and role links are commonly agreed upon (Nelson & Seidman, 1984). Perhaps less metacommunication or role negotiation is required, thus freeing the children to get the show on the road.

Family activities and group programs enable children to develop a large repertoire of common scripts: field trips to the dentist, dairy, airport, library, farm, and many other places broaden children's experiences immeasurably.

Children express emotions in symbolic play

Much of children's play reflects their understanding—or lack thereof—of the world, its objects, roles, and events, according to Piaget (1951/1962).

> Tim is enacting the role of mechanic. When the time comes to repair a tricycle, Tim hesitates. Possibly lacking detailed information on how to make the repair, he simply puts his hands near the handlebar and says "fix." This word seems to have stood for all the fixing details that he could not or did not wish to take time to fill in. (Giffin, 1984)

Piaget viewed such behaviors as arising from inadequate schemes for external reality.

Despite their limited understanding of the world, Piaget attributed to children the ability to transpose reality subjectively in order to serve the ego. He described four types of symbolic combinations that seem to support the mastery of affect:

• *simple combinations*—children construct whole scenes in which reality is changed or imaginary beings are created. A scene may be reenacted with a different, possibly incoherent, order and with some elements selectively omitted. Players do not copy reality, but change it to suit themselves.

• *compensatory combinations*—children correct reality by incorporating forbidden actions into the pretend play. Emotionally charged events may be changed to undo the source of threat, or to create a more desired reality.

> Shiona, age 7, had been told by her mother that she was not old enough to go on one especially appealing ride at the amusement park. She typed her mother a note: "Dear Mom, I'm 8. Now I can go on that ride."

Family activities and group programs enable children to develop a large repertoire of common scripts for pretend play.

Amanda felt left out because she was the only child in her play group who had no brothers or sisters. She invented an imaginary sister and set up a crib in her room for her. Sister had a place at the table and went shopping with the family.

- *liquidating combinations*—children reconstruct an unpleasant situation in a more pleasant context, perhaps so the outcome loses some of its sting. Doctor play, so common with young children, exemplifies this type of play. Children may also reenact traumatic incidents they have experienced, such as a funeral or a dangerous rescue. Thus, like Erikson (1963), Piaget demonstrates how imaginative play can help children gain mastery over trauma.

- *anticipatory symbolic combinations*—an imaginary person disobeys an order and suffers the consequences. One group of preschool children adopted an imaginary person, "Mr. Nobody," who often was blamed for unexplained problems.

In all four of these types of symbolic play described by Piaget, children's emotional health and development are facilitated through role enactment, object substitution, and actions that transpose reality.

Other scholars have offered alternative models to explain the affective nature of this transposition. The script theory proposed by Nelson & Seidman (1984), for example, contends that scripts describe the organization of experiential representations. Scripts are either cognitive (Nelson & Seidman, 1984) or cognitive-affective (Bretherton, 1984; Kreye, 1984) memory models of events.

Fein (1985), however, asserts that this theory fails to provide access to a deep understanding of children's emotions. She asserts that pretend play allows children to think out loud, sometimes collectively, about meaningful experiences—both pleasant and unpleasant. Especially important is children's freedom to alter their relationship to the immediate environment and the freedom to denote things they have not experienced.

Children play with rules in symbolic play Children have no power to change the rules at school, at home, or at camp. But they can change reality through stories and imaginative play.

Bonnie, at the end of a difficult first grade experience with a teacher who pushed her to learn beyond her level of interest, announced, "Mommy, I'm a lawyer now."

"Oh, really?" Mom responded.
"Yes, I'm going to change the laws," explained Bonnie.
"Oh, is that right?" coaxed her mother, curious to learn more.
"Yes, I don't think it should be a law that you have to go to school."

Piaget might have called this assimilation of reality to the ego for the purpose of correcting reality (compensation). Bretherton (1984) referred to imaginative thinking like this as playing "What if?" Bonnie certainly was playing symbolically with changing the rules by playing "What if?"

In symbolic play, rules can be both the object of representation and the source of guidance for the structure of the play, including the social order. Reality can be violated or transformed within certain limits. Even the structure of society may be reflected in children's play. For example, mommies may be allowed to drive the car, but not to fix it.

Rules also guide the play itself. Social rules are used to negotiate roles, and there are rules to maintain the pretend aspects of the play (Giffin, 1984). Thus, children use symbolic play to practice the social rules of the world out of context or to combine them in new ways, all the while using in-frame and out-of-frame metacommunications to state the rules of the play itself (Giffin, 1984).

Children play with rules

Using Piaget's taxonomy of play (practice, symbolic, and games with rules), we can observe children playing with or manipulating rules. The phrase *playing with rules* can be interpreted either to refer to a set of rules which govern the play, or to rules as a resource or target for manipulation (Garvey, 1977). We will now turn to how children's development influences their use of rules in their play.

Rules can be changed　　Rules are statements of stable relationships. Much like the laws of nature, social rules govern interactions. However, if rules or laws are played with, they are either practiced for pleasure or combined in new ways through pretend play. Only in pretend play can elephants fly. Violation of rules in a playful, no-risk context can be funny. For example, when the big powerful Daddy clown in the circus has a bucket of water dumped on him by the small child, it represents a reversal of the rule that adults are always powerful.

Rules have to be understood before they can be the subject of play, however. Piaget (1932/1965) outlined how the consciousness of rules evolves through three levels:
1. Rules are either motoric (don't eat marbles) or not taken as imposing an obligation to apply them.
2. Rules are viewed as sacred (having emanated from powerful adults) and unchangeable.
3. Rules are viewed as law due to mutual consent. Laws are respected, but may be changed if everyone agrees.

In children's play, rules may be practiced repeatedly in a low-risk setting. Later, they may be combined in new ways to create new rules.

> The children in preschool have learned the school routine of free play, then snack, then story, then outdoor play, and so forth. If snack is served at a different time or in a different place, such as on the playground, children may think it is funny.

After the routine is established through practice, children can play around with new combinations. A story told the wrong way won't be silly to a child who is still learning it. Only when the story is familiar will new words inserted in it be funny.

In these examples, reality was changed by creating new combinations in the rules. Later, rules may be changed symbolically in pretend play. Still later, rules that have been viewed as law by mutual consent may be changed (if all agree) to create new rules that govern the play.

Rules govern play   Piaget outlined two criteria for *games with rules*: competition and mutually agreed upon or formal rules to govern the activity. These criteria have been a source of concern to child development specialists. Rubin and his colleagues (1983) point out that if one criterion for play is that it is free of externally imposed rules, then games with rules cannot be classified as play.

Thus, one distinction between play and games with rules hinges on the issue of who imposes the rules. If the rules are enforced externally, then the activity cannot be play. Indeed, a game of Little League baseball may not be playful at all if the focus is on rigidly enforcing the rules or playing only to win. In competition, rules may be imposed to control the level of challenge and to equalize power between competitors. However, if the rules are mutually agreed upon, the rules may be internalized by the players rather than being externally imposed. Also, if a child creates new games and makes up appropriate rules, the rules are not externally imposed.

Another distinction between games and play, according to Ruben et al. (1983), is that one "engages in games to compete, to win, and to achieve some specified goal. One plays for the satisfaction of playing" (p. 728). Again, the distinction appears to be related to whether or not individuals are competing against themselves (to improve their golf score) or competing against others.

Trying to make a simple distinction between games and play ignores the continuous developmental change in our ability to transform rule-governed behavior. The process of rule transformation ranges from implicit in-frame (turn taking) to explicit out-of-frame, formally agreed upon rules, culminating in written rules (laws). Thus it seems plausible that play with rules represents a type of play that undergoes continuous changes along with children's cognitive development. Perhaps if rules of a game are internalized, accepted, and agreed upon, and if the focus is on the process of playing the game rather than winning, then a game with rules may be play. If the focus is on winning, and if rules are rigid and external, the *players* are not players but *workers*.

If the focus is on winning, and if rules are rigid and external, the players are not players but workers.

With maturity children are better able to adapt to external demands, possibly because they gain more power and have more resources through which to meet their ego needs. The powerless child can only achieve power in a pretend situation. Competencies are acquired slowly. It is a gradual process for children to meet ego needs through real world accomplishments.

The realistic models and real skills that characterize the activities of children between the ages of 7 to 11 have been described as the stage of industry (Erikson, 1963). In Piagetian theory, children adapt to reality and thus experience a decline in assimilation (play). School-age children are said to play less. At the same time, they accept the challenge to adapt to the social reality of rules and competition. When they win, their ego needs are met and their accomplishment is recognized as a valuable achievement (industry).

Children acquire the ability to play games with rules gradually. They must remember and coordinate more than one perspective, skills that parallel changes in cognitive and social maturity. They must be conscious of the rules, and remember to apply them while employing a sensorimotor (football) or symbolic (charades) skill.

Following rules is much harder than playing roles because of the need to coordinate cognitive and social demands with sensorimotor skills. Piaget (1932/1965) identified four stages in this process. We will look at how each stage is related to children's development.

Children use materials to practice motor skills or as symbols. For their first 2 years children handle game materials and may play with them in sensorimotor practice or use them as symbols, usually alone.

> For his second birthday, Neal received a rubber horseshoe game set from his Uncle Charlie, who did not realize it would be years before they could play the game together by the rules. Neal explored the rubber horseshoes. He looked at them, and attempted to bend them. Then he pounded them on the floor, and banged them together. Uncle Charlie, eager to play the game, enthusiastically hammered a stake into the ground, and demonstrated how to throw the horseshoe. Neal preferred to play throw and catch. By this time, Uncle Charlie began to see that Neal was not ready to play by the rules. He stopped trying to teach the game and played catch with Neal.

Children's games are egocentric. From the ages of 2½ through 7, children focus on their own actions and do not take into account what other children are thinking or planning to do next. Early games such as Ring Around the Roses quite appropriately involve cooperation and rules for action, but no competition. Therefore, no strategy is needed. The rules tell all players what to do next: "We all fall down." Left to their own devices, children will adapt the materials to fit their needs.

> Elizabeth received a set of playing cards for her fourth birthday. She and her friend Tina played cards by imitating some rules. They divided up the cards, but did so by each picking the cards they liked. They took turns putting cards on the table and picking up new ones. However, there was no effort to win. Each child was essentially playing alone with the goal of compiling a set of favorite cards. Both girls won.

Children cooperate. Between the ages of 7 and about 12, children make an effort to win, and players become concerned that everyone follow the same rules. They may negotiate rules, even while the game is in progress, because rule application is more difficult to achieve than rule consciousness.

Why do children want to change the rules? Some children may need

Following rules is much harder than playing roles because of the need to coordinate cognitive and social demands with sensorimotor skills.

to do so to eliminate the ego threat that comes from losing. Rules can also be changed to get a better match between skills and challenges.

Emily, age 5, wanted to play a competitive racing game with Sarah, age 6. Rules were negotiated and the race began. Midway to the goal, Emily saw that she was about to lose and ran to a different target that was closer to her and farther away from her competitor.

Emily changed the rules in the middle of the game. She was mature enough to be able to negotiate and remember rules, but not mature enough to stand the defeat. Sarah, a year older and more experienced in abiding by mutual rules, was upset. Teachers and parents who observe behaviors like this need to understand that tolerance for competition, rules, and losing is a gradually developing process. How was the problem with Emily and Sarah resolved? In this case, the parents suggested that both girls could win by each running to a different goal. Less sensitive adults may have rigidly imposed the rules and even punished Emily for "cheating."

A group of 7-year-olds at Heather's birthday party want to play Hide-and-Seek. They spend 11 minutes suggesting and agreeing upon the rules—a very serious and nonplayful process. Then they spend about 15 minutes playing the game.

For these children, the rule-negotiation process was still being developed and the rules were not yet incorporated well enough for them to play with changing them. The sensorimotor skills for the game, on the other hand, had been mastered—the group could hide, seek, and run to home base. Through continued peer interaction, children become more flexible about changing rules, especially if the changes make the game more challenging.

Cooperative social behavior is very important, as evidenced in this example. Social experiences such as these gradually lead to better perspective-taking skills.

Children codify the rules. At about age 11 or 12, children reach the final level in which rules known to society are applied. They are interested in negotiating rules. Children are now better able to accommodate to the external demands of reality. Interestingly, many of the games most familiar to children are those that are played, with some variation, in many different cultures: Tag, Hide-and-Seek, Checkers, and Tic Tac Toe.

Chapter four

How Play Relates to Other Behavior

*H*ow does play affect children's social, emotional, and cognitive development? This has been a controversial issue since the play movement began in the United States early in this century, and the heated debate is not likely to subside quickly. Let's look at some of the issues that professionals in early childhood education and child development, as well as parents and the public in general, will probably grapple with for many years to come.

There are indeed many who consider play to be "developmentally trivial and educationally irrelevant" (Rubin, 1980a, p. vii). Montessori, for example, argued that pretend play was pathological, so she designed programs and materials to discourage such play in children.

The argument that play has no value for children appears to be based on the erroneous idea that play contributes little to adult behavior and development. For many researchers, play has been used as a window to study other supposedly more important behaviors, rather than to learn more about play itself.

While play may not be valued in its own right, a glimmer of light exists to uphold the importance of play: the failure of a child to engage in progressively more complex and elaborate play behaviors has traditionally been viewed as symptomatic of disorders in cognitive, social, physical, or emotional development (Tizard, 1977).

Others have argued that play is a significant force in children's development and have designed programs based on the natural play behaviors of children. We are just beginning to understand the adaptive role of play and other behaviors in preparing children for adulthood (Hole & Einon, 1984; Martin, 1984).

Part of the problem in defining the rewards of play derives from the fact that we are trying to track down the benefits of an enormous and diverse category of behavior. Asking about adaptive significance of play is rather like asking about the significance of "goal-oriented" behavior. (Wolf, 1984, p. 183)

Much of the work discussed in this chapter was conducted in an effort to establish the value of play by tying it to the development of behaviors already highly valued in children: cognitive, social, and emotional. However, keep in mind that we should value play not just for its indirect stimulation of cognitive skills and problem solving but because play is the main feature of what it means to be human (Vandenberg, 1985).

We should value play not just for its indirect stimulation of cognitive skills and problem solving, but because play is the main feature of what it means to be human.

Play contributes to cognitive development

High quality preschools, child care centers, nursery schools, and other early childhood programs have long accepted the value of play in young children's learning. In contrast, play has been included only sporadically in the public school curriculum, reflecting the changing purposes and philosophical orientations that determine the direction of public education.

Until recently, when empirical evidence became abundant, early childhood educators justified the inclusion of play in programs with theoretical and philosophical arguments. At the same time, misconceptions of what play is about, and abuses of play in programs for children, have abounded. Play has received a great deal of bad press.

With the advent of public-supported preschool programs such as Head Start, and the tremendous growth in the need for child care, the preschool curriculum has become a public issue. It is now subjected to many of the same influences, expectations, and pressures made on public school systems (Elkind, 1986; Glickman, 1984). Many of today's parents, in response to the widespread stress on cognitive development in children, are demanding that their children be exposed to a program that is more than *just play*. Parents may choose a program for its so-called academic focus. In response, programs often include the terms *school, early learning, academy,* or some such phrase in their names.

While many parents and teachers know how valuable play is for young children, many more are unaware of its role in promoting children's development. We in the field of early childhood education/ child development have not been diligent enough in sharing our knowledge and experience about play. Consequently, many programs have succumbed to misguided pressure and use direct instruction rather than play.

Research alone, in which we document how effective play is for learning, is not without its dangers. By focusing on how play can increase cognitive gains, we may overlook the merits of play as an activity in its own right. Also, if we only concern ourselves about academic development, we may neglect how valuable play is in other areas of development. Already we know that social and aesthetic activities are necessary for children to develop to their greatest potential. To tangle the issue further: Although research shows that play is related to problem solving and creativity, these abilities are not highly valued in the current climate of pushing "back to the basics."

In light of all these complications, play is not likely to become a part of the public school curriculum and may even lose its place in preschools unless both professionals and the public reconsider the purposes of education (Glickman, 1984). Perhaps this book will lead teachers, parents, principals, curriculum specialists, school boards, and other decision makers to take a more balanced look at the kind of people we want our nation's children to become. Let us begin by elaborating on just how play can contribute to children's learning.

We have already seen in this book how children's play progresses through increasingly higher levels of abstraction and sophistication. Children's cognitive maturity is evidenced by their increased ability to discriminate relevant from irrelevant information (needed for problem solving); a decrease in the number of cues needed to generate information; and an increased capacity to communicate and express their needs, thoughts, and feelings through symbolic activities (Athey, 1984).

Research and theory about how young children learn show us that play contributes to learning and cognitive maturity in a number of ways:

1. Play provides the opportunity for children to practice new skills and

functions. As they master these activities, they can integrate or reorganize them into other task-oriented sequences. Babies learn to turn the pages of a book and begin to sense a sequence to the story. Books become lifelong friends when children begin to learn about them in a playful manner.

2. Play offers numerous opportunities for children to act on objects and experience events—it gives children a wide repertoire of experiences. Each field trip, each friendship built with children and adults including some from different cultures, each experience in building with blocks builds understanding about the world.

3. Play is an active form of learning that unites the mind, body, and spirit (Levy, 1978). Until at least the age of 9, children's cognitive structures function best in this unified mode. Watch how intense children are when they paint at an easel, work on a puzzle, or gaze into another's eyes.

4. Play enables children to transform reality into symbolic representations of the world. For example, children may be bowling and decide to keep count of how many pins each knocks down. Tokens or paperclips may be kept in a pile, or older children may want to write the numbers on paper.

5. Through play children can consolidate previous learning. Much of what we learn cannot be taught directly, but must be constructed through our experiences. We all know the feeling of "Ah-ha!" when something finally clicks.

6. As they play, children can retain their playful attitude—a learning set that contributes to flexibility in problem solving. Children are open to a variety of solutions. They are amazingly inventive in solving problems such as how to get an enormous Halloween pumpkin from the bus to their room: roll it, pull it in the wagon, find someone strong enough to lift it, use a derrick, drive the bus up to the door and push the pumpkin in, carve it first to make it lighter, or chop it up and give everyone a piece (solutions don't always have to be workable!).

7. Creativity and aesthetic appreciation are developed through play. When children see how difficult it is to work with clay they can appreciate the efforts involved in sculpture and pottery. As they play with words, they develop a sense for the rhythm and sonority of poetry and prose.

8. Play enables children to learn about learning—through curiosity, invention, persistence, and a host of other factors. Children's attention spans are amazingly long when they are interested. They are entranced as they watch an anthill; they keep trying until the puzzle is solved; they delight in having recognized their own name for the first time! Children become self-motivated learners.

9. Play reduces the pressure or tension that otherwise is associated with having to achieve or needing to learn. Adults do not interfere. Children relax. Play provides a minimum of risks and penalties for mistakes. Have you ever seen a child who wanted to stop playing?

Play reduces the pressure or tension that otherwise is associated with having to achieve or needing to learn.

Play encourages problem solving

Play and exploration, as we have seen, are often inseparable. Both are linked, by research and theory, to children's abilities to solve convergent and divergent problems. *Convergent* tasks are those that have a single, correct solution, whereas *divergent* tasks have multiple solutions. These two types of thinking may represent different modes. First let us look at children's convergent thinking.

Research in this area is growing. In a typical task children are asked to retrieve an out-of-reach object and, in order to do so, must figure out how to join two or more sticks together to make one long enough to reach the lure. One group of children in the experiment is given the opportunity for free play, in which they are allowed to play with the sticks and joining devices. Other children are given a demonstration of how to use the joining devices. A third group, called the control group, is given the task without the benefit of either free play or a demonstration.

Results from such studies consistently show that children in the free play group perform better than the demonstration groups on other problem-solving tasks given to them after the one with the sticks (Cheyne & Rubin, 1983; Smith & Dutton, 1979; Sylva, Bruner, & Genova, 1976; Vandenberg, 1981b). Of course, each study is designed differently, and it is only logical that success is also related to the

Play enables children to learn about learning—through curiosity, invention, persistence, and a host of other factors.

children's ages. Nevertheless, play clearly helps children whose abilities are well matched with the demands of the convergent-thinking task.

Play and its relationship to divergent thinking has also been researched (Dansky, 1980a, 1980b; Dansky & Silverman, 1973, 1975; Pepler & Ross, 1981; Sutton-Smith, 1968). This research, investigating linkages between play and creativity, has been hailed as some of the most promising work on children's creativity in the last decade (Kogan, 1983).

Studies on divergent thinking are similar to those used to assess the relationship between play and convergent thinking. Children in the play group are given a set of materials, such as pipe cleaners and paper clips, and told to play with them in any way they wish. Other children are asked to watch an adult perform several tasks with the materials and then to repeat what they saw demonstrated. All the children were then given a task testing *ideational fluency* (the nonevaluative association of a wide variety of schemata and the capacity to focus on more than a single aspect of the situation). They were asked, for example, to name all the things they could think of that are red. Children in the play groups consistently outperformed children in the other groups. This research supports theories about the similarities between symbolic play and ideational fluency. Play is thought to contribute to ideational fluency because it gives children a wide set of experiences upon which to draw associations and because it establishes a playful learning set.

Not all play activities are equally effective in enhancing divergent thinking, however. In one study, children who were instructed to make believe with the materials provided gave more original responses for an unfamiliar object than children in the free play and control groups (Li, 1978).

In another study, children given divergent experiences (puzzle pieces) generated more responses on a fluency measure than children given convergent experiences (puzzle pieces and the form board) (Pepler & Ross, 1981). Perhaps divergent play experiences generalize better to many problem-solving situations, whereas learning through convergent experiences applies only to very similar convergent problems.

Children's behavioral styles and personalities may also contribute to their performance on these tasks. Playfulness traits (social and cognitive spontaneity, manifest joy, and sense of humor) have been significantly correlated with performance on measures of ideational fluency

(Lieberman, 1965; Singer & Rummo, 1973). Similarly, children who have a predisposition to engage in make-believe play or exploration benefit more from play experience that preceeds divergent problem-solving tasks (Dansky, 1980a; Hutt & Bhavnani, 1976). Imaginative and social fantasy play have also been related to ideational fluency (Johnson, 1976; Moran, Sawyers, Fu, & Milgram, 1984).

Several studies report that free-play opportunities are more effective than play training on convergent and divergent problem-solving ability (Dansky, 1980b; Feitelson & Ross, 1973; Rosen, 1974).

Teachers and parents must also be aware that specific types of adult interaction and the materials offered may have a detrimental effect on divergent thinking (Moran, Sawyers, & Moore, in press). To examine the effects of structure in materials and instructions on preschoolers' creativity, Moran and colleagues first assigned children to one of four groups: structured instruction with either structured or unstructured materials, and unstructured instruction with either structured or un-structured materials. In a subsequent session, the materials were re-versed but the type of instruction remained the same. The materials for all groups were sets of small plastic building blocks, with wheels included in the structured set.

An adult was present in all sessions, but in the structured instruction session demonstrated how to build either an airplane or a truck, and then asked the child to build the same object. Although this was really only a demonstration with modeling, when this instruction was com-bined with the structured materials, children were less flexible in ideational fluency. In other words, with the simple addition of wheels, children were unable to shift their thoughts from category to category as easily.

Many other variations on this theme have been tried in an effort to assess the effects of play training, and it is difficult to compare results. Some studies use sociodramatic play experience, sociothematic tuto-rials, or playing pretend roles with adults. The number and frequency of the training sessions vary from one session to weekly sessions for several months. Measures of the outcomes are diverse, as are the samples of the children involved. And of course the results are further complicated by the fact that no distinction is made between play and exploration.

Despite all these complications, the evidence indicates that play, regardless of whether it is spontaneous or the result of training, en-hances performance on divergent thinking tasks (Kogan, 1983).

These findings seem to lead to the conclusion that play is preferable to direct instruction in promoting children's convergent and divergent problem-solving abilities. Yet, it is important to keep in mind that play was not always necessary for children to produce the correct solution on convergent tasks or to perform well on ideational fluency tasks. Many children performed well on these tasks without the benefit of the specific play experience provided in the study. Perhaps future researchers need to learn more about children's previous experiences (structured preschool vs. free play curriculum, parents' style of interacting with the children) to better evaluate the effects of play on problem solving.

Play supports children's language and literacy The mystery still has not been solved: How does symbolic usage in play and language emerge? Much attention has been given to uncovering the role that play has in the acquisition of language (Cazden, 1974; Kirshenblatt-Gimblet, 1976). The similarity in the development of the use of symbols in language and in pretend play has been widely recognized (Athey, 1984; Garvey, 1977, 1979; Giffin, 1984; McCune-Nicolich & Bruskin, 1982; Pellegrini, 1984; Sachs, 1980).

Perhaps children's ability to use symbols is related to their interactions with adults, through which they come to realize that some actions are to be taken literally while others are not (Sachs, 1980). Perhaps the skills of metacommunication develop in the course of peer play "to meet the need for interpersonally communicating and negotiating complex, internal images of what should happen" (Giffin, 1984, p. 74) in assuming the multiple levels of role taking. Indeed, observations of language-delayed children reveal that they tend to play alone more often (McCune, 1985).

While research indicates that the development of symbolic usage in play and language is related (McCune, 1985; Nicolich, 1977), it is not clear if that relationship is due to symbolic maturation, to personal style, or to the expressive functions of language.

Children's first attempts to read and write frequently occur during play. Studies of early readers reveal that these children play a great deal. Dramatic play, as compared with functional and constructive play, appears to be associated with better reading and writing skills in kindergarten children (Pellegrini, 1980).

Other studies show that children trained in sociodramatic play do better than children in other conditions (such as discussion groups) on story comprehension and on recall of an unfamiliar story (Pellegrini & Galda, 1982; Saltz, Dixon, & Johnson, 1977; Saltz & Johnson, 1974). Although play is not a necessary condition for learning language and literacy skills, play is probably the best environment for these abilities to thrive.

Play furthers social and social-cognitive abilities

Among all the areas in which play is recognized as beneficial, perhaps the development of social skills is the least controversial. Research has been conducted in two related subareas:

• *social skills*—children's ability to manage the environment through cooperation, helping, sharing, and successful social problem-solving, and

• *social cognition*—children's ability to think about their social world (Rubin, 1980b).

One of the most potent sources of information for children is other people—other children in particular. Much of their play is based on socially learned rules and experiences. Many scholars contend that pretend play is related to and/or contributes to the development of a variety of social and social-cognitive skills (Bretherton, 1985). Others, notably Piaget, view play as a reflection of the child's social and cognitive functioning.

The often-cited theoretical link between play and social functioning is derived from Piaget (1970), who believed that children are intrinsically motivated to engage in social interactions. Conflicts between peers arise because children are egocentric. When children resolve these conflicts, they learn how to competently manage the environment. If the children agree while they play, play is primarily assimilation. When there is a disagreement, accommodation is necessary as children move out of the play frame to negotiate the conflict. Thus through play children move beyond their own egocentricity and expand their knowledge of the social world.

Children who engage in pretend play are able to decenter—to think about more than one viewpoint or thing at a time. This ability to decenter is inherent in many social skills as well and has been a popular source of investigation by child development researchers.

Children's frequency of social pretend play predicted their social

Children's first attempts to read and write frequently occur during play.

competence, popularity, and role-taking ability in one study (Connolly, 1980). Similarly, in another study (Rubin & Maioni, 1975) results indicated that children who engaged frequently in dramatic play scored high on classification and spatial perspective-taking tasks, whereas children who engaged frequently in functional sensorimotor play scored low on the same measures.

When children are trained in sociodramatic play and/or fantasy, their scores have been found to increase on a variety of measures of

- perspective-taking ability (Burns & Brainerd, 1979; Matthews, Beebe, & Bopp, 1980; Rosen, 1974; Saltz & Johnson, 1974; Smith & Syddall, 1978),

- group cooperation (Rosen, 1974; Smith & Syddall, 1978),

- social participation (Smith, Daglish, & Herzmark, 1981), and

- impulse control (Saltz et al., 1977).

Other researchers found that sociodramatic play training had little or no effect on children's social skills (Brainerd, 1982; Connolly, 1980).

Why are these results contradictory? Certainly the type of play training varies. It could be that in some studies the findings were a result of the adult attention rather than of the play training per se. Even so, in one study concentrating on the adult interaction, children given fantasy play training outperformed children in other treatment groups on a role-taking task (Smith & Syddall, 1978). The effects of sociodramatic play training also appear to be relatively long lasting (Smith et al., 1981).

The positive benefits of social play continue to be documented. For example,

> when parents and infants are playful and enjoy their interactions with one another, infants are more likely later to be securely attached, to enjoy problem-solving tasks, and to be sociable with adults and with peers. (Beckwith, 1985, p. 157)

In expanding on Beckwith's work, Fein (see "Discussion" in Beckwith, 1985) suggests that secure attachment between 12 and 18 months results when infants acquire a measure of affective self-regulation through parent-infant play. Children who are securely attached by this age are then able to move on to engage in play with peers and thus develop further social skills to manipulate and organize their environment.

Much of what occurs in children's sociodramatic play is based on social relationship factors within the group such as friendships, the dominant status of the group, and familiarity with play themes (Rubin, 1985a).

In a longitudinal study of children from preschool through first grade, Rubin and his associates (1985a) used social play to identify children at risk for socioemotional problems such as depression and anxiety. We will look at this research in detail, as it is rich with implications for parents and teachers.

Children whose most frequent play was solitary-functional and children who engaged frequently in the less sophisticated types of play (solitary-dramatic, parallel-functional, and parallel-dramatic) performed less well on social and interpersonal problem-solving tasks. These same children were rated as socially incompetent by their teachers and were observed to be rejected by their peers.

In contrast, popularity, social competence, perspective taking, and social problem-solving skills were observed in preschool and kindergarten children who frequently engaged in sociodramatic play. In addition, parallel-constructive play for these age groups was positively related to peer popularity, higher teacher ratings of social competence, and better interpersonal and social problem solving.

As might be expected, the highest level of play, games with rules (Rubin et al., 1976), was the category of play most strongly associated with peer popularity, social competence, and social cognitive development in kindergarten and first grade children.

Children in Rubin's study were characterized as isolate, average, or social. The three groups were described this way:

1. Isolate children produce more transitional, "off-task" activity than their more sociable age-mates. They are also less boisterous in their play.

2. . . . Withdrawn preschoolers engage in more solitary-functional and solitary-dramatic play than others but in an equal amount of solitary-constructive play. . . .

3. . . . During group play, the sociable children are more likely than isolates to participate in dramatic play and games. . . .

4. Extremely withdrawn children do not receive significantly more negative sociometric ratings than children in other groups, though teachers rated preschool isolates as more fearful and anxious than others.

5. On a social problem-solving measure (see Rubin & Krasnor, [1986]), isolate children produce fewer alternative solutions and are more likely to suggest "adult intervention" strategies than their more sociable age-mates.

6. Isolate children are more likely than average or sociable children to talk to themselves or to an imaginary playmate during free play with another child.

7. When isolate children direct requests to another child, they tend to be "low-cost" (e.g., "Look at this"). Even so, isolates experience less compliance to their directives than do other children. Furthermore, when their requests fail, isolate children are less likely than sociable ones to modify their original strategies. (Rubin, 1985a, pp. 92–93) (Reprinted by permission of Johnson & Johnson Baby Products Company)

When Rubin followed up on his study, he found that 60% of the children originally classified as isolates retained that status. Stable isolate children were found to be as popular with their peers as more social children and were equally successful in two problem-solving

Play provides the context for role and rule conflicts with peers, thus setting the stage for children to practice and consolidate their social skills.

tasks. However, the stable isolates rated themselves as less socially, academically, and physically competent than did their peers. Furthermore, as Belsky notes in Rubin (1985a), it appears that these socially withdrawn children were avoiding social contact rather than expressing a greater interest in the nonsocial world.

Another interesting contrast emerging from this study is that aggressive-rejected children are radically different from withdrawn children. Aggressive-rejected children appear to have an inflated ego, which leads them to externalize social-cognitive problems, while withdrawn children seem to be lacking in self-esteem.

In light of all these findings, it appears that play provides the context for role and rule conflicts with peers, thus setting the stage for children to practice and consolidate their social skills.

Children express emotions during play

Until recently, positive affect was often included in the definitional characteristics of play—we believed children always have a good time when they play. However, play may not always be a pleasant experience (Sutton-Smith & Kelly-Byrne, 1984). A more contemporary view of play may be that children practice with pleasure the negative feelings or anxieties, as well as the positive feelings, associated with real-life events (Beckwith, 1985). For example, illness and picnics are common play themes, yet one is an unpleasant and the other a pleasant experience (Fein, 1985).

The emotional aspects of children's lives as expressed through pretend themes have been given little attention by researchers. Play has been linked to healthy emotional functioning primarily through the work of Freud and his followers, who view play as a medium for expressing feelings that children may or may not be able to verbalize. Although psychoanalytic theorists agree that pretend play arises from both internal and external demands, there is no consensus on whether these demands are based in past experiences or are the result of more general age-related sources (Fein, 1985). Much of the psychoanalytic literature concentrates on trauma, and yet recent work indicates that pretend play is more often framed around everyday episodes rather than around specific traumatic events (Fein, 1985).

Children practice with pleasure the negative feelings or anxieties, as well as the positive feelings, associated with real-life events.

Play is also associated with an understanding of self—a necessity if children are to express themselves. Play provides children with the opportunity to examine themselves and their relationship to the environment in a comfortable way and at a self-paced rate. Thus, through play children feel able to control their world and their feelings.

Unfortunately, the value of play for normal emotional development and self-control has received little research attention, but the few studies done indicate that play supports emotional functioning.

Other researchers have examined the benefits of symbolic play on behavior. Children who engage in imaginative play have been found to be able to wait longer, an indication of greater impulse control (Singer

& Singer, 1979b). When children reenacted fairy tales, their performance was facilitated on a reflective thinking task and on several tests of
impulse control, while children who engaged in free play with familiar
themes did not perform as well (Saltz et al., 1977).

Children who are playing are usually seen as competent, at ease,
familiar, and in a positive mood. Indirect support for this notion can be
drawn from informal observations of children in hospitals and other
unfamiliar settings—they do not play when their anxiety level is too
high.

Play may also reflect children's thoughts, anxieties, and fantasies.
Teachers long ago learned to exercise caution believing that all of a

*Play can facilitate healthy development. Play may even provide
the best context in which children grow and learn.*

child's play reflects the child's own experiences! Many themes or
episodes may arise from movies or television, for example.

Adults must also be cautious in assuming that all play is good play.
When children repeatedly relive a traumatic event, such behavior may
not be play, and may even maintain or heighten tension rather than
reduce it. At that point, professional counseling is recommended.

Play is a very effective method to diagnose, assess, and treat children
with dysfunctional behaviors, even though a great deal of professional
judgment must be made in the absence of specific data or measures. For
example, we do not know the normal range, let alone the best levels, of
different forms of children's play.

Although play therapy is widely used as a nonthreatening and
enjoyable medium for intervention, it only makes sense that not all
types of play training, experience, or therapy are appropriate for all
children. For example, fantasy play is not appropriate for schizo-
phrenic children who cannot distinguish between fantasy and reality
(Nahme-Huang, Singer, Singer, & Wheaton, 1977).

When the play therapy process is examined, we find a pattern of
behaviors that occur over a period of time (Guerney, 1984). These
results give us further insight into the value of play for emotional
development and functioning. At first, the emotions of disturbed children are diffuse and undifferentiated, generally negative, and out of

proportion or exaggerated. With time and through play, their feelings become more differentiated, more directed, and more reality oriented. After a period of ambivalent feelings, positive and realistic feelings emerge in the final stages of play therapy.

For those interested in further exploring the application of play in other settings, we recommend these readings:
Play in hospital settings—Bolig (1984); Lindquist, Lind, & Harvey (1977); Wilson (1985)
Play in therapy and clinical settings—Bentovim (1977); Diantoniis & Yawkey (1984); Guerney (1984); Kalveboer (1977); Miller (1984); Trostle (1984)
Children with exceptionalities—Cicchetti (1985); Confer (1984); Mogford (1977); Quinn & Rubin (1984)

Summary

Although play is probably not essential for children to develop various cognitive, social, and emotional skills and abilities, the research clearly indicates that play can facilitate healthy development. Play may even provide the best context in which children grow and learn. In the next chapter we will look more closely at the myriad of factors that can influence children's play.

Chapter five

Factors That Influence Play

*C*hildren do not play in a vacuum. As parents and teachers, we know that we can make a difference in children's play by how we interact with children and arrange settings in which children are inclined to play. Before we decide how to facilitate children's play, we must understand what factors provide the context for play (Darvill, 1982). In reviewing the literature, we find that the key components of a good play setting for young children consistently include:

• an array of familiar peers, toys, or other materials likely to engage children's interest;

• an agreement between adults and children, expressed in word, gesture, or established by convention, that the children are free to choose from the array whatever they wish to do within . . . limits . . .;

• adult behavior that is minimally intrusive or directive;

• a friendly atmosphere designed to make children feel comfortable and safe; and

• scheduling that reduces the likelihood of the children being tired, hungry, ill, or experiencing other types of bodily stress. (Rubin et al., 1983, p. 701)

From this list, you can see that the play environment has many components, both physical and social, that interact with each other as well as with the children's developmental levels and individual differences—no wonder such a wide variety of play behaviors has been observed! And no wonder that various types of play arise from or are affected by different combinations of all of these factors. We now turn to a closer look at how individual children interact with their environment to create diverse play settings.

Children make a difference

In every group of children at play, we can observe similarities and differences in children's levels of development, individual styles, and social backgrounds.

Development sets the parameters Until children have the physical, cognitive, and socioemotional capabilities required to play in a particular way, no amount of stimulation from the environment can make it happen. Maturation sets the upper limits of children's play behavior. For example, no toddler is capable of playing games with formal rules—and yet people who are unaware of children's capabilities persist in offering inappropriate toys such as the set of horseshoes Uncle Charlie gave his nephew. Both the structure and the style of children's play become more diverse and more complex as they mature (Fein, 1979), as we saw in previous chapters.

Each child is different We now know that each child actively determines what happens in play and other interactions. Have you ever met a really charming, animated baby who inspired you to be just a little silly? Or, on the other hand, have you ever encountered a sober, lethargic baby who left you wondering what to do next because nothing seemed to interest the child? People of all ages determine what happens to them in many situations, and play is no exception. Of course, children can only use, make, see, touch, or imagine objects and events that match with their experiences in their environment.

There are many ways we can think about pretend play and its relationship to the individual and the environment. Perhaps, "with respect to human development, pretend play marks the transition from stimulus-dominated behavior to organism-dominated behavior" (Fein, 1981b, p. 261). Fein believes that the interaction between the physical environment and the child occurs on several levels. On one level, the interaction takes the form of "stimulation as a sensory or motivational experience and reality as a cognitive experience" (p. 176). At another level, the interaction takes the form of "stimulation and reality as they are organized, remembered and transformed in the mind" (p. 276). A third level consists of the overlap between these two levels.

*Until children have the physical, cognitive, and socioemotional
capabilities required to play in a particular way, no amount of
stimulation from the environment can make it happen.*

Children are selective.   Every child has favorite toys and people—
and every child's favorites are different. Children tend to select those
things that fit with their past experiences and that are organized,
transformed, and remembered over time. You might want to try to
remember or find out what your favorite toys were as a child and reflect
on why you may have made those choices, or talk with some young
children about their toy choices.

It seems that individual differences in interests and functioning
develop when children are given the opportunity to repeat, practice,
and expand certain behaviors. Without this support—from objects and
people in the environment—children would be unable to select these
activities. We know, for example, that infants who are stimulated are
more likely to seek further stimulation as they grow (Sutton-Smith,
1979).

Infants as young as 6 months appear to take a role in eliciting appropriate and stimulating play materials, and thus the cycle begins. Toys that offer children just the right amount of stimulation lead children to higher levels of social and personal adjustment. In turn, these

> children with better cognitive and social skills appear to elicit from their parents greater cognitive stimulation (including the provision of more advanced toys and materials)—in sum, the maintenance of a more nearly optimal environment. (Bradley, 1985, p. 132)

Children's toy selection is probably related to their needs at the moment (Lewin, 1935). An engaging toy is a source of satisfaction, while one that is too simple or complex is not. The appeal of a toy varies with children's development and their mood.

Children must be in the mood. Play is more likely to occur when children are in a moderate mood or state of arousal rather than when they are intensely aroused. For example, after surgery, children usually refuse to play with toy surgical tools for about a week.

Mood seems to be affected by children's sense of security. Children are more anxious, but display more exploratory behavior, when they are in new play settings rather than in familiar ones, and they are more likely to explore when others are near than when they are alone (Hutt, 1976). Toddlers who are securely attached to their mothers tend to explore more than children who are not securely attached (Matas, Arend, & Sroufe, 1978). Undoubtedly, there are many other factors that affect children's mood to play.

Children's play styles vary. Our discussion in this book has centered around developmental differences in children's play, in part because so little is known about children's individual play styles (Krasnor & Pepler, 1980). Nevertheless, we know that individual traits make a difference in children's play—the amount of playfulness, sensitivity to the environment, and how the environment is used to support the play (Dansky, 1980a; Feitelson & Ross, 1973; Lieberman, 1965). Again, think of children you know, or the child you were, and how readily observable these styles are.

Surely these individual differences account for some of the confusing and sometimes even contradictory results of the best research. For example, as children mature, their propensity both to engage in dramatic play (Johnson & Ershler, 1981) and to explore (Hutt & Bhavnani, 1976) appears to be stable. Discovery of "the course of development [of play], with all its individual variety, multilinearity and mobility of operations" requires study of the process of change through the lives of individuals (Sutton-Smith, 1985, p. 66).

Individual differences in symbolic play styles have been explored in some depth (Shotwell, Wolf, & Gardner, 1979; Wolf & Grollman, 1982). Independent of changes in development, it seems there are two distinct styles of players: *patterners* and *dramatists*.

Patterners devote most of their time to explorating and manipulating objects. When they make object substitutions in fantasy play, the substitution is based on realism or physical similarity. Once they make a substitution it is continued through the play episode. For instance, if a patterner substituted a crayon for a nail, the crayon would remain a nail for as long as the play episode continued, and would not be used in other substitutions.

Dramatists, on the other hand, use objects as props for social interaction. They maintain fantasy themes for long periods of time, even incorporating background noise and other potential distractions into their play. Object substitutions are not limited by physical similarity, and the same object may be substituted for a variety of things in the same episode. A crayon might serve as dog food, a walkie-talkie, and a watch, for example, in the play of dramatists.

Sex differences exist.   Sex differences have been noted in the play of children as young as 12 months. For example, throughout early childhood, boys' play seems to be more boisterous and competitive, and usually lasts longer. Boys tend to play in large groups with blocks and movable toys in motor play. Girls are more likely to engage in social play in groups of two, using art materials and preferring dramatic play (Hartup, 1983). Parallel play is twice as frequent, and cooperative play four times more likely, with same-sex playmates than with opposite sex peers in children aged 4 years (Serbin, Tonick, & Sternglanz, 1977).

Other consistent sex differences have also been found in boys' and girls' play. Toy preferences differ between sexes (Carpenter, 1979) as do the types of roles played (Hurlock, 1971; McLoyd, 1983; Sanders & Harper, 1976; Stone, 1971). For example, McLoyd found these differences in roles:

	Boys	Girls
Type of role		
fantastic	40%	6%
occupational	32%	19%
familial	28%	75%

Less consistent sex differences have been found in the amount and complexity of cognitive (Rubin, 1977) and social (Smith, 1977) play forms.

All of these results are probably complicated by factors such as differences in adult behavior, types of toys available, and ratios of girls and boys (Serbin & Connor, 1979). Indeed, the number of mixed-sex interactions can be increased by reinforcing such interactions (Serbin et al., 1977), and other forms of play undoubtedly are also strongly influenced by adult attitudes and other environmental factors.

Social backgrounds play a part. Culture plays a key role in children's play. Complex cultures with high demands and high levels of stress, such as in the United States, have more play and more games. In authoritarian societies, children's play tends to be primarily imitative, whereas in more open societies children are free to attempt a variety of possibilities and therefore their play is more transformational (Sutton-Smith, 1979). If you find these differences fascinating, you can learn more about the anthropological work on cultural differences in children's games and rules in Schwartzman (1978).

Culture plays a key role in children's play.

Children from low-resource homes may play differently than children from higher income groups. Low-resource children tend to exhibit less fantasy play, less diversity and variety in fantasy roles, less frequent verbal expression of make-believe, and fewer object transformations in fantasy play. They are likely to engage in more solitary and parallel functional play and less constructive play (Feitelson, 1977; Feitelson & Ross, 1973; Smilansky, 1968).

Taken together, these findings seem to indicate that preschool and kindergarten children from low-resource backgrounds exhibit less mature forms of play than children from homes with more resources. However, the ideas of social class and income are so broad that these findings are not very helpful in determining why or even whether these children really play in different ways (McLoyd, 1985).

The assumption has long been made that low-resource children did not play due to restrictive conditions in their homes resulting in an inadequate play environment. There are so many variables, however, that the evidence is inconclusive. In fact, some results indicate that there is no difference between groups, and that the development of more complex play in low-resource children is delayed, rather than nonexistent, as suggested by earlier investigators (Schwartzman, 1984). Clearly, a great deal more work needs to be undertaken in this area.

The environment sets the stage

When children's play erupts into arguments, violence, or other disruptive behaviors, parents and teachers most often assume the children are the cause of the problem. We may be overlooking the real source of conflict—the social or physical environment. Once we are aware of how these factors determine the course of children's play, we will be able to take steps to establish or design more productive play environments for young children.

When children's play erupts into disruptive behaviors, we most often assume the children are the cause of the problem. We may be overlooking the real source of conflict— the social or physical environment.

The social environment sets the tone   Children's play is affected by their relationships with other people: families, teachers, and peers. The way we treat children and our attitude toward play make a difference in children's play. Interestingly, researchers in the fields of psychology and anthropology have concluded somewhat independently that the role adults model and the protection they offer are the most important prerequisites for children's play (Sutton-Smith, 1979). Whether parents or teachers, adults play a key role in children's play.

Parent-child interactions.   Several longitudinal studies have focused on whether interactions between parents, particularly mothers, and their children affect children's development. It appears that parent involvement and the provision of play materials are the two most "potent and pervasive" influences on children's cognitive development (A.W. Gottfried, 1985b).

Little research has been done to determine how different childrearing patterns affect play. One study indicates that parents of highly imaginative children hold imaginative play activities in high regard, acknowledge their children's play rather than join in, and facilitate play indirectly through secure relationships.

In a study of children in the early stages of adjusting to a divorce, the play seemed to be less mature and less sophisticated than for children in a group not recently affected by divorce. Boys seemed to be affected more than girls (Hetherington, Cox, & Cox, 1979).

As we have already noted, the findings regarding family resources and parent attitudes and practices toward play are inconclusive (McLoyd, 1985).

Mothers (and other caregivers as well) vary greatly in the amount of sensitivity they display toward their infants' play behaviors. In order of increasing sensitivity, three distinct styles can be identified:

1. *Unrelated*—the mother changes both the toy and the action in the play activity. Her responses and actions are not based on the child's behavior. Rather, she imposes her actions and the toy on the child.

2. *Imitative*—the mother simply repeats the child's action with the toy.

3. *Elaborative*—the mother takes into account the relationship between the child's action and the toy and modifies one of them. She introduces variation while keeping the task simple (Fein, 1979).

This elaborative style appears to be very fragile. Levenstein (1985) noted that if the parent insists on the child's learning, the child becomes bored, the exchange breaks down, and the interaction is no longer playful. She concluded that "the probability is that mothers who approach the young child's learning through play with spontaneous joy will have a child who continues to find joy in learning" (p. 165). Surely the same holds true for caregivers in other settings as well—church schools, group child care, family day care, and nursery schools, for example.

Differences in the level of involvement, the type of play activities, and the style of interaction between mothers' and fathers' play are of great interest here as well (Porrata-Doria, 1984; Rubin et al., 1983). For example, some adults enthusiastically participate in pretend play, while others actively discourage it (Dunn, 1985).

Research indicates that, in general, fathers spend less time than mothers with their children, but fathers spend a higher percentage of that time playing. Fathers tend to engage in rough-and-tumble play, unusual play, and parallel play with their infants.

In contrast, mothers usually engage in conventional games such as Peek-a-Boo, read to their children, or manipulate a toy to directly stimulate the child, depending on the child's interest in exploring. They point and demonstrate to help the child focus attention on the object and explore (Belsky, Goode, & Most, 1980). Mothers use play to discuss the functions and appropriate uses of objects, as well as concepts such as size and shape—in short, they are didactic (Dunn, 1985). Mothers' pretend play often revolves around a nurturing theme (shopping, cooking) and frequently involves discussions of people's feelings (Dunn, 1985).

Additionally, conversational style and social class may account for differences in adult interaction with children. For example, working-class mothers tended to associate pretend play with lying and therefore discouraged it in their children (Dunn, 1985). Perhaps parents, fathers in particular, are hesitant to join as equal partners in their children's play because they view their role as one of a powerful socializing agent (see Vandenberg, in "Discussion" in Dunn, 1985).

Influence of siblings. Researchers repeatedly find that many play behaviors first begin in the context of mother-child or sibling-child interactions at home (Fenson, 1985). While mothers are often spectators or teachers, siblings are likely to be equal partners in play (Dunn, 1985). Pretend play with siblings is more fanciful than that with mother. Some of the favorite themes include trips to the moon, undersea adventures, and monster play.

Teacher-child interactions. Other research has looked at how teachers influence children's play. One study found that 37% of all teacher-child interactions occurred in the art area, while only 17% occurred in the block and doll corners where most pretend play takes place. Yet children spent 37% of their time in the block and doll areas, and only 21% engaged in art activities (Shapiro, 1975).

What do observations like this mean? They could mean that the art activities required more supervision. Or they might indicate a difference between adult and child interests—the adults preferred art activities (Phyfe-Perkins, 1980). Another interpretation of these results is that they reflect children's development, in that children's social activity with adults decreases steadily throughout childhood (Fein, 1981a). And perhaps the teachers were knowledgeable about how best to support pretend play! Once children are comfortable with the environment and with playmates, research indicates, adults should interfere as little as possible if children's play is to be fostered (Rubin et al., 1983). These teachers may have just been doing their job well!

Peer influences. The relative social position, ages, and familiarity of playmates can make a great difference in children's play. It has long been assumed that children's social and cognitive competencies depend upon their interactions with other children as well as adults.

When 4-year-olds were asked with whom they preferred to play— playmates or parents—children's most frequently answered their parents (Strom, 1981). Why? Because with their parents, they said, they could be the boss! Parents do indeed sometimes give in to young children in an effort to equalize the power. However, peers and older siblings are less likely to let a younger child dominate the play.

Play relationships between adults and young children have been called *metacomplementary*—a relationship that is defined as symmetrical but is in fact asymmetrical (Schwartzman, 1979). Other types of relationships in children's play behaviors include:

- *asymmetrical dyads*—parent(s)-child, older sibling-younger sibling;

- *asymmetrical group relationships*—teachers-children, older children-younger children;

- *symmetrical dyads or groups*—friend-friend [same age]; and

- *group confrontations*—good guys versus bad guys (Schwartzman, 1979, pp. 250–251).

Children's roles in dramatic play are undoubtedly affected by their relative social position. The less popular, more withdrawn, and younger children play the roles that are low on the hierarchy of roles (such as pets or babies) (Rubin, 1985a; Schwartzman, 1979).

The age range in a group of children and their familiarity with each other also influence their play.

Mixed age interaction can be viewed as a context for the socialization of asssertiveness (both prosocial and antisocial) and for seeking assistance from others. Same-age socialization can be viewed as a context for acquiring skills needed in "give-n-take" in both pleasant social exchanges and aggressive ones. (Hartup, 1983, p. 109)

In other words, both loose neighborhood groups with a variety of ages of children and organized programs with more limited ages have positive and negative influences on children's behavior!

In general, children display more advanced behavior when they play with older children than when they play with others their own age. Older children tend to use less complex speech when they play and talk with younger children. Age differences may affect the quality and quantity of play even when children know one another (Brownell, 1982). Schwartzman (1985) has even gone so far as to argue that same-age groups of peers are not universal and may even be maladaptive. Throughout history, multiage groups have been more common. This argument surely deserves reflection when planning programs for young children.

In some circumstances, familiarity of play partners may be more influential than the children's ages (Hartup, 1983). For example, children are more likely to use objects in a nonliteral way when they are with a familiar playmate than when they are alone (Rubenstein & Howes, 1976). When a friend is present, children's fantasy play is likely to be more complex (Matthews, 1977, 1978) and to last longer (Doyle, Connolly, & Rivest, 1980).

> One child commented to her mother that it was hard to use her model horses in play with new friends because they did not know the characteristics of each horse. (Sachs, 1980)

Perhaps these findings are in part due to children's shared information about the toys. Familiarity with the setting as well as with the children appears to influence play. When children are in an unfamiliar environment, they pay more attention to toys; at home, they are more social (initiate interactions, extend interchanges, and act aggressively) (Becker, 1977; Jeffers & Lore, 1979).

A toy's color, form, or complexity cannot elicit sustained play as well as peers can (Ellis, 1979). Other children are truly the greatest source of complexity. Even when children play alone, they prefer to be able to see other children at play (Campbell, 1979). Attention spans are longer when children can see others at play—a definite argument for more open play areas, rather than small, private spaces. Which leads us into a closer look at the physical environment.

The physical environment provides the props The quantity and quality of toys and materials children have, and the amount and arrangement of space, all make a difference in the way that children play.

Toys and materials—what difference do they make? The number of children's toys helps determine how, or even whether, children interact with each other. In general, in the absence of toys, children as young as 6 months of age turn to each other for stimulation (Ramey, Finklestein, & O'Brien, 1976). Without toys, children's social interactions are more sophisticated and more coordinated, and extend over longer periods of time. Similar results have been reported for older preschool children.

However, before you conclude that toys are not necessary, you need to be aware of one other fact: When toys are not available, the number of aggressive acts increases (Johnson, 1935). Except in severely overcrowded conditions, low availability of toys accounts for more conflicts over toys and other aggressive acts than does the amount of space (Smith & Connolly, 1976; Smith & Green, 1975).

Attention spans are longer when
children can see others at play.

Even the size of the toy has been shown to affect the type of social interactions in children's play (DeStefano & Muller, 1980). More negative interactions were observed when toddlers were given small manipulative toys (cars) than when they played with large immovable toys (slide/boat combination).

The type of toy or activity can also make a difference in the types of social and cognitive play interactions. Dress-up clothes, cars, and other small vehicles are the basics for preschoolers' pretend play. In contrast, paints, crayons, and scissors elicit nonsocial constructive play. Nonsocial functional play results when children are offered clay, sand, and water. Indeed, the presence of art materials seems to inhibit the occurrence of social pretend play (Rubin & Seibel, 1981).

In studies that span several months, the types of play that children engage in with different materials varies little, with one exception: blocks. Play with large blocks changes from functional to constructive. Children playing together with the blocks tend to engage in pretend play. In contrast, solitary play with blocks tends to be constructive.

Clearly parents and preschool teachers can indirectly control children's free play simply by their selection of materials and activities (Rubin & Seibel, 1981).

This is also true for older children. When 7-year-old children were given isolate toys (gyroscope, crayons, Tinker Toys™, jigsaw puzzle, Farmer Says™, Talking Book™, and clay), social play occurred 16% of the time. When they were given social toys (Don't Cook Your Goose™, Don't Break the Ice™, Don't Spill the Beans™, Pick Up Stix™, checkers, and playing cards), social play occurred 78% of the time.

Toys that demand specific tasks tend to elicit the behavior for which they were designed. As we saw in Chapter 4, children given divergent play materials (puzzle pieces) exhibited more divergent thinking on subsequent problem-solving tasks than did children who were given convergent play materials (puzzle pieces and their form board). Children who were given the convergent play experience were more likely to try the same solution over and over again on subsequent problem-solving tasks (Pepler & Ross, 1981).

One study compared children enrolled in a Montessori program (where the focus is on didactic materials that have only one correct use) with children in a traditional early childhood program (that encourages multiple uses of toys). As might be expected, the Montessori students were more task oriented (Dreyer & Rigler, 1969).

Children benefit from novelty, complexity, and variety. We still have a great deal to learn about which characteristics of toys elicit and maintain children's exploratory play (Nunnally & Lemond, 1973). Most of the studies that have been done used experimental stimuli rather than real toys in real play situations. Based on this experimental work, it appears that novelty or uncertainty about an object increases exploratory play. Most parents and teachers are aware that children are easily enticed by a new toy—this distraction technique works well in many situations! However, some evidence also suggests that novelty may inhibit children's imaginative play (Hutt, 1976).

Complexity of toys and materials can also influence play (McCall, 1979; Nunnally & Lemond, 1973). Very complex toys seem to elicit exploratory play, while functional and symbolic play are more typical with toys that are moderately complex. Perhaps this helps explain why children often are more interested in the box than the complex new toy that comes inside of it!

Variety of toys is also positively associated with children's cognitive development (Gottfried & Gottfried, 1984; Ulvund, 1980). Variety not only facilitates the transition between exploration and play, but also provides numerous opportunities for children to deal with cognitive discrepancies that probably advance cognitive functioning (A.E. Gottfried, 1985). Many toys have a limited life (rattles) because they are soon outgrown, while a few (unit blocks) seem to grow with the child.

Not nearly enough attention is paid to the change in objects over time. This is important, because it relates to the whole notion of match or optimal discrepancy. . . . I think what variety does, both short-term and long-term, is maximize the probability that the child will be able to select objects that are optimally discrepant for this child. Obviously as a child gets older if there is no change in objects this probability is reduced. (Wachs, 1985, p. 51)

How do these findings apply to group programs for young children, or even to homes? Although stimulating materials are found in every program, there is little variety from program to program—most good programs have the same toys and equipment (Caldwell, 1985). Another problem is that in some programs the same toys are always available, rather than being rotated. With repeated exposure to the same toys day after day, week after week, children get bored with the toys to the point they don't even see them.

The optimal environment for learning is not too strange, nor is it too familiar.

Similarly, while different homes may have different selections of toys based on parent tastes, most parents are probably inclined to leave all of the toys out all of the time, and soon children complain they have nothing to play with. Most adults can attest to children's delight when a toy that was thought to be lost is found—their interest is renewed!

Wachs (1985) has pointed out that variety is related to the problem of the match that Hunt (1961) identified, and that has become so well known—the optimal environment for learning is not too strange, nor is it too familiar. And who makes this match? Parents and teachers "can provide variety, but the child is the only person who can solve the problem of the match" (McCune, 1985, p. 52). Of course, adults who are observant are well aware of when children are ready for more complex toys and activities, and they respond by providing appropriate materials.

Other factors such as responsivity and availability of toys are also important. Toys that respond to children's actions (activity boards, musical instruments) seem to motivate children to master the skills involved (Jennings, Harmon, Morgan, Gaiter, & Yarrow, 1979; Yarrow, Morgan, Jennings, Harmon, & Gaiter, 1982). Toys that are readily available also seem to enhance children's cognitive development (see reviews by Bradley, 1985; Wachs, 1985). If children do not have easy access to toys, chances are the toys will be ignored. That is the primary reason why toy boxes are the worst possible places to store children's toys—out of sight, out of mind.

As we have seen, if toys and play spaces are not provided, children play aggressively with each other. If items other than toys are available, they will use them like toys and create their own play spaces (Schwartzman, 1985). Infants can amuse themselves in the grocery store with a set of keys; preschoolers can play with a huge empty box for hours on end.

Some people fear that if toys are available, children will use them rather than their own imaginations. However, "there is no evidence that modern children are either more or less creative with their current 'plastic' playthings than were their predecessors with bits of wood or stones" (Sutton-Smith, 1985, p. 62). Even when props and toys are available, children in one study used their imaginations in about half of their pretend play (Matthews, 1977).

How can you determine whether children have an adequate variety of toys and play environments? You may want to consider using the checklist developed by Kritchevsky and Prescott (1977). The checklist is based on the fact that complexity, variety, and the number of activities are related to children's attention span, group participation, dramatic play, nondisruptive free choice of activities, and goal-directed behavior. In this framework, equipment or toys are ranked in the level of complexity.

- *Simple* materials have one use—swings, for example.

- *Complex* toys or equipment have subparts or entail two different types of materials—a sandbox and sand toys, for example.

- *Super units* are comprised of three or more different types of materials—dress-up clothes, for example.

The higher the level of complexity, the greater the number of available activities per child—this is the measure of variety. The amount to do per child can then be calculated using the number of play spaces per child. An interesting project might be to compare the cost of simple items with the cost of those that are more complex. This may help you decide how to get the most play value for your money.

What about structured and realistic toys? The popular belief is that highly structured toys inhibit pretend play and creativity—both

Highly structured, realistic toys tend to facilitate pretend play in children younger than 3½.

important facets of children's development. Much of the research in this area has focused on didactic toys, those designed to teach one concept, and on highly realistic toys.

The results of work in this area are mixed, indicating that the dichotomy between high structure and low structure is too simplistic. Structure also appears to function differently in different types and levels of imaginative play. Children's age seems to play a big part, too.

In general, highly structured, realistic toys tend to facilitate pretend play in children younger than 3½. However, children make more object substitutions with low structure toys. Once again, moderation seems best, and children should probably be provided with a wide variety in the structure of their toys.

Television probably hampers a child's creativity and imagination in much the same way as highly realistic toys (Singer & Singer, 1979a). Children who watch more television are often less imaginative in their play. Although television viewing with an adult is preferable to children watching alone, Singer and Singer (1976) found that imaginative play increased more when children were taught make-believe play than when they watched television with or without an adult. Similar concerns have been raised about whether computer toys and games, video games, and other devices will have a similar effect on children's play. This research is just now emerging (Kee, 1985).

How are toys related to intellectual development? In reviewing the research on the relation between play materials and intellectual development, we can draw some conclusions. Some clearly are more tentative than others:

- Young children tend to spend a considerable amount of time viewing and interacting with toys and other objects.
- There is a moderate correlation between the availability and use of toys and children's mental test scores beginning as early as the second year of life.
- The relation between play materials and intelligence appears to be reciprocal with brighter children eliciting more appropriate play materials to interact with.
- Part of the observed correlation between toys and intellectual development may reflect their joint relation to family social status and parental encouragement of development, but the total relationship does not seem attributable to these factors.
- Toys and other objects frequently serve as the focus of social encounters—more fully social as the child matures. Such encounters afford numerous opportunities for direct and incidental learning.
- Toys and other physical objects appear to have an inherent attractiveness for young children. They draw children into action and serve as a source of skill development and tool mastery.
- Toys can serve as a catalyst for imaginative play and can serve to carry the meaning of the play situation to full realization. They may also help to provide a link between learnings derived from the imaginative world of play and the more concrete settings of the real world. (Bradley, 1985, pp. 139–140) (Reprinted by permission of Johnson & Johnson Baby Products Company)

How does space affect children's play? Physical space clearly must be arranged to support the developmental needs of children and the goals we have for them (Prescott, Jones, & Kritchevsky, 1967). Conflicts between children, as well as between adults and children, can often be alleviated by a carefully thought out arrangement of the physical space. Furthermore, new and more advanced forms of play can be stimulated by changing the placement of toys, equipment, and furniture.

Few attempts have been made to measure environments for young children (Phyfe-Perkins, 1980), although licensing codes generally include square feet per child as one requirement. Density has probably received the most research attention. McGrew (1972) is credited with making a distinction between social density (the number of people in a space) and spatial density (the amount of space available for a constant number of people). Unfortunately, most research has not been based on this distinction. It is difficult to compare studies because so many different methods have been used. We will, however, attempt to summarize some of the most important recent work.

As the amount of space decreases, the level of social interaction, including aggression, increases (Hutt & Vaizey, 1966; Smith & Connolly, 1972). As mentioned earlier in this chapter, this increase in aggression may also be due to the limited number of toys and activities. When space is reduced, rough-and-tumble play and running decrease, while physical contacts increase.

In contrast, other research has shown that crowding results in fewer social interactions (Hartup, 1983). Friendship and imaginative play are more common in small groups than in large ones in classrooms ranging in size from 10 to 25 children (Smith & Connolly, 1980). Young children are more likely to interact in groups of two than in larger groups (Bronson, 1975; Vandell, 1977). With increasing age and maturity, children appear better able to handle large groups (Hartup, 1983).

Although the results from the National Day Care Study (Ruopp, Travers, Glantz, & Coelen, 1979) indicate that the single most important factor affecting the quality of child care is the teacher-child ratio, this factor has been overlooked in the studies of crowding. As we have seen, young children prefer small groups. Therefore, simply providing more adults to achieve a desirable teacher/child ratio without also considering a limit on total group size seems unwise.

We are familiar with one kindergarten in which 60 children shared one very large room. Even with two teachers and two student teachers, this group size was not appropriate. Many rules and limits had to be imposed just to maintain order. You can imagine the noise, traffic congestion, and problems with transitions in managing such a group, not to mention how difficult it was to carry out a worthwhile educational program!

Outdoor space also affects children's play. Traditional playgrounds (containing fixed, conventional equipment) elicit functional play, whereas creative playgrounds (with a variety of mobile equipment) foster pretense play (Campbell & Frost, 1978). Constructive play is rare on both types of playgrounds, although it is the most common form of indoor play (Rubin et al., 1983). These findings point out the need to provide children with both indoor and outdoor play daily.

A reassessment of children's outdoor play areas seems to be in order as well. Certainly no large investments should be made in playground equipment without defining goals for children's outdoor play and thoroughly studying the type of environment needed to reach those goals.

Physical space and materials can be arranged to facilitate children's behaviors, although no specific models have yet been identified due to the complex nature of the preschool environment (Phyfe-Perkins, 1980).

What are the effects of different curricula on children's play? Some curriculum models, such as Montessori and DISTAR, are highly structured, while traditional early childhood programs have been more child oriented. Each curriculum model has very different goals for children, and there is a great variability in how the models are actually implemented in practice. In addition, children's families play a major role.

Even with all these complications, in general, we can conclude that highly structured preschools foster constructive, goal-directed, manipulative play, whereas less structured programs encourage dramatic and functional play.

Given the association between parallel and constructive play and between interactive play and functional or dramatic play one may infer that less structured programs would favor higher levels of social play. High levels of teacher direction may decrease opportunities for peer interactions and an emphasis on convergent learning may not be as valuable as an emphasis in divergent learning experience for the development of important social skills. (Johnson & Ershler, 1982, p. 141)

Readers interested in learning more about how different program models affect children's play are encouraged to explore the wide variety of research available (Beller, Zimmie, & Aiken, 1971; Dreyer & Rigler, 1969; Huston-Stein, Friedrich-Cofer, & Susman, 1977; Johnson & Ershler, 1981; Johnson, Ershler, & Bell, 1980; Miller & Dryer, 1975; Rubin & Seibel, 1979; Tizard, Philps, & Plewis, 1976a, 1976b).

Highly structured preschools foster constructive, goal-directed, manipulative play, whereas less structured programs encourage dramatic and functional play.

Summary

Some of the research findings about the influence of the environment on children's play are inconclusive. However, from the results we have cited, and from the observations and experiences of parents and teachers for many years, we have accumulated a great deal of practical knowledge. We know that children's development establishes the parameters of play. We know that the social environment can either foster or inhibit play, depending upon attitudes and relationships. And we know that the availability and variety of toys, materials, and activities determine to a great extent how children play.

Now we are prepared to bring all that we know about children's play together to make recommendations for parents and teachers.

Children need both indoor and outdoor play.

Chapter six

Ways To Encourage Play

*T*his is the chapter many of you have been waiting for—practical suggestions, for your children or those you teach, based on research, theory, and experience: how to select toys and materials, how to design environments, and how to interact with children in ways that will facilitate their learning through and enjoyment of play.

We will offer these suggestions based on the types of play identified in Rubin's Play Observation Scale (1985b), which you will recall is based on the work of Parten (1932), Piaget (1951/1962), and Smilansky (1968). These categories have endured for many years; they provide a framework for thinking about the basic dispositions of play, its context, and developmental issues specific to each type of play. Each of these types of play can occur as solitary, parallel, or group play. Some resources for additional information are listed so you can pursue topics of interest to you.

How to foster children's functional play

Most of young children's first play experiences, and many play activities of older children, take the form of functional play: They enjoy the sensory stimulation from simple repetitive activities. Infants bang a spoon on their highchair, toddlers climb on everything in sight, 3-year-olds ring the bells on their tricycles, 4-year-olds pour sand from hand to hand, and 6-year-olds swing on tire swings—all of these activities are functional play. At times, functional play gives children a chance to master skills; at other times, their play may reduce tension or relieve boredom. And always, of course, it is fun for the child.

Basics for functional play

You can easily provide the few basics that children need to engage in functional play. A little forethought and a lot of creativity will serve you—and the children—well.

• *Toys or other objects should function properly.* The jack-in-the-box handle should turn and make noise, and Jack should pop up. Telephones should jingle when dialed. The strings for beads should be tipped for easy threading (shoelaces work fine for this). Check toys often to make sure they work.

• *The environment must allow children to play safely without undue verbal and physical restrictions.* An easy way to make sure children's play areas are safe is to get down on your hands and knees, notice everything that children might get into, and then make it safe. Homes and classrooms for infants and toddlers should be childproofed: For example, put locks on cupboard doors, store poisons in locked cabinets, plug electrical sockets, use gates to block stairs, and store precious breakables until the child is older. Remove poisonous plants. Make sure floors are not slippery. Older children also need you to watch out for their safety. If your play area is in the basement, make sure there are no exposed hot water pipes, for example.

Toys and equipment also must be matched to the child's skills and ability to understand. Be creative about what you offer children to play with—expensive toys are not a necessity. Infants can have a delightful time with old magazines, toddlers love to climb on piles of soft pillows, 5-year-olds enjoy climbing in trees. Offer many different types of items, too, and don't restrict yourself to what you find in the toy store.

The best musical instruments for young children are those they can shake or strike—tambourines, maracas, or triangles, for instance. Infants can pour water, while older children will enjoy sand. As children grow, continue to alter the environment so they can play without too many restrictions. Take every step possible to make sure you don't have to say "No!" to protect children.

How to set the context

Adults make it possible for children to engage in and enjoy even the most simple play.

• *Be sensitive to and responsive to children's play.* Notice what children are doing and comment on it. "Oh, listen! Beth is making a song when she taps the stick on the floor. What a nice beat!" You can even offer to extend children's play if they are interested. "Rajan, would you like some cups to use at the sand table? Or do you need some water?" Your interest and encouragement will reinforce children's self-motivation and pride in their play.

Your interest and encouragement will reinforce children's self-motivation and pride in their play.

• *Offer toys that provide sensory stimulation or feedback.* What sights or sounds will happen when your child plays with the toy? Can baby see the smiling face in the mirror? Can the pegs be pounded into the carpenter bench? Does the dough clay feel cool and soft on the hands? How does the music make you want to move?

• *Take children outdoors to play.* Every child needs fresh air, sunshine, and a chance to run and shout. Not only are children who play outdoors healthier, but, as we have seen, they tend to play differently outside. Most babies love to ride in the stroller and watch the neighborhood sights—tall buildings, flowers, blowing wind chimes, or bustling crowds.

Vary the outdoor setting, too, from playgrounds to open fields to woods, and move typical indoor activities out on a beautiful day. Wagons to push and pull, bubbles to blow, shadows to jump on—a whole new world awaits children outside. And have a picnic, or at least a snack, outdoors often!

Keep children's development in mind   • *Have enough toys.* Until the age of 3, children cannot be expected to share. Children will naturally learn to share when (1) people are generous with them, and (2) there are enough toys so other children will not snatch favorites away. Arbitrary methods of forcing children to share do not work. Children learn to be generous with their friends when they don't have to hoard toys and when they feel confident their needs will be respected. Therefore, duplicates of popular toys are essential for infants and toddlers in group programs.

Older children also need a sufficient number of toys so that everyone has something to use, materials can be rotated to eliminate boredom, and the variety is sufficient to appeal to children with different levels of development and interests.

Don't wait for children to ask—anticipate what comes next!

• *Match toys and equipment to children's development.*   Observe children carefully to see what items seem to offer just the right challenge, and when children have mastered skills and are ready to move on. Babies who can crawl need safe places to pull themselves up to standing—perhaps a footstool or coffee table with rounded edges. When children can match all the shapes in the shape sorter, they are ready for puzzles with more pieces. When they can ride tricycles well, a bicycle with training wheels is the next step. Children first learn to paint with thick, bright tempera colors and wide brushes on large blank paper at the easel. As their muscle control develops, smaller brushes, smaller papers, thinner paints, and even watercolors might be in order. Don't wait for children to ask—anticipate what comes next!

Resources for ideas about functional play
Baker, K.R. (1966). *Let's play outdoors*. Washington, DC: NAEYC.
Cherry, C. (1971). *Creative movement for the developing child: A nursery school handbook for non-musicians*. Belmont, CA: Pitman Learning.
Hill, D.M. (1977). *Mud, sand, and water*. Washington, DC: NAEYC.
McDonald, D.T. (1979). *Music in our lives: The early years*. Washington, DC: NAEYC.
NAEYC. (1985). *Toys: Tools for learning*. Washington, DC: Author.
Sullivan, M. (1982). *Feeling strong, feeling free: Movement exploration for young children*. Washington, DC: NAEYC.
Sutton-Smith, B., & Sutton-Smith, S. (1974). *How to play with your children (and when not to)*. New York: Hawthorn/Dutton.

Ways to encourage constructive play

Children's intentional building or creating with objects or materials is classified as constructive play in Rubin's framework. Constructive play is the most frequently observed type of play among 3- and 4-year-olds, perhaps because of the large number of common early childhood toys that elicit this type of play: art materials, blocks, puzzles, and manipulative toys such as plastic building blocks. Many woodworking, cooking, and science experiences also provide opportunities for constructive play.

Basics for constructive play
• *Emphasize the process rather than the product.* This will aid in developing children's creativity, but even more importantly will ensure that children feel competent and good about their own work—and therefore will be self-motivated to continue to learn. How do you keep the focus on what children are doing, rather than on the end result?

First, avoid the use of adult models of art or building projects for children to copy. Put simply, do not use dittos and coloring books. Do not cut out patterns so children's artwork all looks alike because all they have to do is paste it together. Likewise, don't build something with Legos™ and expect children to copy your example. Rather, let children use materials in ways that are most meaningful to them.

Let children use materials in ways that are most meaningful to them.

Secondly, talk with children about *how* they made their creation: "You stirred and stirred that batter to make it just right." "Ribbon, lace, and felt—what a variety of textures you have included on your collage!" Adults are often tempted to praise children's work ("What a good painting!"), to ask "What is it?" and even to set up art contests. These external judgments soon become meaningless to children. Sometimes everything everyone does receives a similar response from adults, and children soon tire of the message. Young children do not always make "something" and should not be forced to label their constructions. Tailor your comments to the child's emerging sense of worth and developmental level. See Schirrmacher (1986) for some excellent suggestions about talking with children about their art (or any other constructions).

• *Help children take advantage of opportunities to solve problems and think divergently.* So much formal schooling seems to focus on finding the one right answer and how to use things the one right way. Life is rarely like that, however. Scientists, architects, artists, com-

Allow children to solve their own problems rather than interfering to offer your solution. Give them the opportunity to try some unworkable solutions, and let them choose what works best for them.

puter programmers, parents, drivers, budget planners—all of us are faced every day with problems that have many solutions. We want children to learn to think divergently as a way of life.

How can we do this? Rather than probing for one specific answer, encourage children to try out, or think of, multiple solutions. Ask questions focusing on "what if?" and "how can we . . .?" rather than those with a yes, no, or other specific response.

Keep limits as broad as possible without compromising children's safety or wasting resources. Instead of insisting that children keep the white dough clay separate from the red, allow and even encourage them to experiment with what happens when the two colors are mixed. Then keep on using the pink dough!

Allow children to solve their own problems rather than interfering to offer your solution. They may have a better idea! When two children both want to use the puppet stage, let them negotiate a solution, perhaps for time-sharing or collaborating on a play. If a group wants to build a bridge with unit blocks, encourage them to come up with several ways to span the river. Give them the opportunity to try some unworkable solutions, and let them choose what works best for them.

These kinds of experiences give children background knowledge about objects, events, and people. They can use what they learned— and how they figured it out—all their lives.

How to set the context   • *Signal to children that it is OK to be messy.*   Get involved yourself with the finger paints. Offer a wet sponge calmly to a child who has spilled the glue. Have a broom and dustpan available at the woodworking bench. Leave ample time for children to clean up when they have finished. If necessary, have children wear smocks to protect their clothing.

• *Add more and more complex materials as children become more capable.*   Toddlers will be content with a few different sizes and shapes of unit blocks, but 5- and 6-year-olds will need large quantities, quadruple lengths, and arches for their complex constructions. Large-scale plastic blocks are great for 3-year-olds, but older children have the fine motor skills it takes to work with tiny ones. Spreading cream cheese is a super beginning cooking activity, while older children can delight in planning, shopping for, and cooking complicated ethnic dishes.

• *Store materials so they are accessible.*   Sturdy, open shelves make it possible for children to find what they need and to put it back where it belongs. Toys are less likely to be broken or lost when stored on shelves. You can even use picture labels on the shelves to help children locate the proper spot for art materials, puzzles, blocks— everything.

• *Provide ample periods for children to select their own activities.*   Constructive play is not likely to happen when all the children are doing the same thing in one large group. Throughout the

Sturdy, open shelves make it possible for children to find what
they need and to put it back where it belongs.

day, large blocks of time should be scheduled in which children can choose what they want to do and then carry through with their ideas without fear of interruption. Similarly, children should not be expected to rotate from one center activity to another on a predetermined schedule. Rather, in the course of time, children will take the opportunity to select from a broad range of types of activities during free play.

How does this work in a classroom? Group sizes can be limited, if necessary, for each activity. You can talk with preschool and school-age children to determine together how many children will comfortably fit in the housekeeping area or the block corner. Popular special experiences, such as cooking, may need to be offered for several days until all children who are interested have had a chance to participate.

Sometimes new props will need to be introduced to entice children into the area or to stimulate more advanced play. Often an adult's presence alone will draw a crowd.

Keep children's development in mind Regardless of the play material, children generally progress from object-dominated exploration to child-dominated creations. Also, when first presented with something new, children and adults alike explore its physical properties and experiment to determine its potential. Children's art development offers a good example of how development progresses throughout the early childhood years.

When a toddler is given a crayon for the first time, she or he may taste it, bang it, and eventually discover that it can make marks (exploration). With experience and advancing motor development, children progress through a series of levels of scribbling (functional play). At the next level, children begin to label drawings after they have been completed (fortuitious combination), calling the circle a sun or Mommy. Then, with more experience and maturation, children determine in advance what realistic pictures they intend to draw (anticipatory combinations). Children's development through these stages varies, but generally their focus switches from the process to the product at about the age of 8 or 9. Until then, our focus with children should also be on the process, and everything we say and do should value what children are doing, not what they have made.

Resources for ideas about constructive play
Cherry, C. (1972). *Creative art for the developing child*. Belmont, CA: Pitman Learning.
Hirsch, E.S. (Ed.). (1984). *The block book* (rev. ed.). Washington, DC: NAEYC.
Lasky, L., & Mukerji, R. (1980). *Art: Basic for young children*. Washington, DC: NAEYC.
Manning, K., & Sharp, A. (1977). *Structuring play in the early years at school*. London: Ward Lock Educational in association with Drake Educational Associates.
Schirrmacher, R. (1986). Talking with young children about their art. *Young Children, 41*(5), 3–7.
Skeen, P., Garner, A.P., & Cartwright, S. (1984). *Woodworking for young children*. Washington, DC: NAEYC.
Wanamaker, N., Hearn, K., & Richarz, S. (1979). *More than graham crackers: Nutrition education and food preparation with young children*. Washington, DC: NAEYC.

Always support symbolic play

In Chapters 2 and 3, we focused on children's fantasy play: assuming the role of another, substituting or imaging objects, enacting events. Infants begin by acting out daily routines. Preschool and school-age children have reached the level of maturity where this type of play is common. It contributes to their cognitive, language, and socioemotional development, and therefore should be supported both at home and in groups.

Basics for symbolic play • *Support, but never force, pretend play.* A few dress-up clothes, books such as *Caps for Sale,* or other props are usually all that is needed to get children interested in make-believe. It is such fun no rewards are needed, just opportunities to enjoy.

• *Give children control of their make-believe play.* Unless safety is a concern (children want to play Superman by leaping from the top of the slide), children's pretend play rarely needs any interference. If you spot a way to extend play (perhaps children need help to incorporate a new player or to get their barking dog to go to bed), assist gently and then step aside gracefully. If you play *with* the children, maybe joining them on a train ride, take your cues from the children and get off at a convenient stop.

• *Resist temptation to impose order on children's pretend play.* Children's symbolic play, like their constructive play, centers on the process. Their play has no first, second, or third acts (and no intermission, either). Let children define what happens and when. If they want to act out a story, let them determine its course, variations and all. What about performances in which children memorize lines or follow a script? Absolutely not. Children's play is necessarily their own—it doesn't belong to you or even the world's greatest playwright!

• *Act playfully yourself!* Ordinary activities are always more interesting with a little pretend—Mary Poppins's spoonful of sugar. Broccoli pieces are a thrill to eat when they are trees being devoured by beavers. If cleanup time is meeting with resistance, perhaps you can find some pirates to help put the gold nuggets (crayons) into their secret treasure chest.

Throughout the day, large blocks of time should be scheduled in which children can choose what they want to do and then carry through with their ideas without fear of interruption.

• *Encourage children's involvement.*   Children new to the group
or those who are less socially capable may need a bit of assistance to
join in. Maybe the circus needs clowns or someone to sell hotdogs.
Offer a prized prop, such as a firefighter's hat, and see how the child's
confidence soars when a fire suddenly breaks out.

• *Pretend doesn't have to be real.*   Make-believe does not have to
be an exact imitation of reality. Children may change the order or
characters of a story, or have a pet that does magic tricks. Dinner may
be served first thing in the morning, and consist solely of ice cream
cones. Who cares? This is a time for children to alter reality and
express their wishes and anxieties.

---

*Children's pretend play is necessarily their own—it doesn't
belong to you or even the world's greatest playwright!*

How to set the context   • *Choose appealing props.*   Hats, rep-
                                      licas of food, suitcases, stethoscopes, a
                                      beach towel, a cash register—each one of
                                      these items can be the basis for a whole
variety of themes upon which children can build. Adults just offer the
appropriate props. A pad of paper and a marker can be incorporated
into nearly every theme. Use your imagination and pick up on the
children's cues! You might want to store props specific to themes in
separate boxes for easy retrieval. Why not bring out the picnic box in
January!

• *Build on children's experiences.*   Field trips, books, holidays,
visitors, and children's everyday activities with family and friends
form the basis for pretend play. The broader children's experiences are,
the more likely they are to expand on interesting themes in pretend
play. Listen to what children talk about and find ways to incorporate
their ideas.

• *Watch for when you are needed.*   As we noted earlier, sometimes an adult is needed to head off an aimless episode or redirect a
repetitive theme. You might need to participate, or sometimes just
elaborate. Other times you can facilitate the play. Carefully observe
what children really need, and then offer just enough to get them on the
right track.

• *Minimize interruptions.* Just as with constructive play, children need long periods of time in which to carry through with their ideas. Plan the day so that time is available. Play areas can also be arranged to reroute traffic or define space. Clearly you don't want everyone walking through the block corner on the way to the restroom. Children who are trying to read books probably will not appreciate the continued conversation in the housekeeping area. Plan the room arrangement, and the placement of all shelves and tables, with traffic flow and noise factors in mind. Tents, lofts, and boxes may be one answer in tight spaces—they can be transformed into castles, monster caves, or space colonies.

Consider children's development

• *Be prepared to pretend with baby.* Children's earliest attempts at symbolic play require a willing and playful adult as well as realistic props. Older infants and toddlers are most likely to start by playing typical daily routines—eating, sleeping, dressing, bathing. When you see baby turning the steering wheel, you might comment "Beep, Beep! Here comes Melissa!" Give children a chance to play with their combs or their washcloths. Join gleefully in a game of Playing Possum.

• *Change your style as children grow.* With experience, children become less dependent upon adults and turn to their peers as play partners. They also require less realistic props and their themes become more elaborate. Your role now is primarily to keep adding to children's experiences with trips, books, visitors, and opportunities to explore a variety of materials.

The broader children's experiences are, the more likely they are to expand on interesting themes in pretend play.

• *Let the children direct their play.* Young school-age children may want to produce dramas, making up the script as the play progresses. Sometimes stories or movies serve as the basis for these plays. On occasion, a teacher or parent may need to offer a prompt or lead, such as "And then . . ." or "Who is that knocking at the door?" Older children may even want an audience. Perhaps children in after-school programs can put on a play for the preschoolers in the group. Participation should be entirely voluntary, and the play should be allowed to evolve as it goes—no memorized lines. Sometimes a musical will emerge. Or puppets may be painstakingly created. Offer your support by providing what children need to fulfill their ideas.

- *Challenge children to extend their play.* Without imposing your ideas, you can prompt children to experience higher levels of symbolic play. Perhaps some of the more realistic toys are rotated to the closet, so children must select other items to substitute for their play. You might want to review the levels of pretend play described in Chapter 3 to know just how much discrepancy to introduce!

Resources for ideas about symbolic play
Hunt, T., & Renfro, N. (1982). *Puppetry in early childhood education.* Austin, TX: Nancy Renfro Studios.
McCaslin, N. (1975). *Act now! Plays and ways to make them.* New York: S.G. Phillips.
Sutton-Smith, B., & Sutton-Smith, S. (1974). *How to play with your children (and when not to).* New York: Hawthorn/Dutton.

Provide games with rules

In Chapter 2, we found that Piaget (1951/1962) characterized children's games with rules as those play activities that are competitive and that are bound by pre-established limits or rules. The competition may be with another person or with oneself, and the rules may be conventional or made up by the participants as the game goes along.

Most of us have fond memories of playing games with our friends or families, and we are eager to share these traditions. There are many different types of childhood games, such as aiming, racing, chasing, hiding, guessing, following verbal commands, playing cards, and board games (Kamii & DeVries, 1980). Some typical preschool games are Lotto, concentration or memory games, Hide and Seek, and Who Spilled the Beans?

While games with rules do not fit the criteria for the definition of play unless the children make up the rules, all games can certainly be approached with a playful attitude.

Basics for playing games with rules We have seen how important it is for children to be self-motivated to play games and to enjoy themselves during the game (rather than playing only to win). These suggestions will help you guide children's game playing.

• *Keep participation voluntary.* You may suggest a game, but children should never be forced to take part.

• *Modify the rules to keep children active.* For example, if children want to play musical chairs, find a way to involve everyone. For 3-year-olds, you may want to have the same number of chairs as children. If the competition causes older preschool children to feel left out, perhaps everyone can continue playing with just one chair fewer than the number of children. If children are eliminated in the traditional way, have an alternative activity ready for them.

• *Select a variety of games that offer opportunities to master social, cognitive, and motor skills.* Children derive a great deal of pleasure from exercising and combining their skills. Some games give children a chance to understand mathematics (Chutes and Ladders™, Dominoes, or any game requiring scorekeeping) or improve their early reading skills (Go Fish, Lotto). Some involve color recognition (Candy Land™), while others require physical skills (Ring Toss). Still others focus on strategies (Chinese Checkers) or cooperation (Dodge Ball; relay races; Button, Button).

• *Choose games in which feedback is apparent to the children.* Games such as Bingo give clear evidence of children's progress. Races and relays help children see how well they can do. Older children will be pleased when they figure out their opponent's strategy in Checkers.

• *Avoid offering prizes or special privileges for winning.* These will undermine children's intrinsic motivation to play. Adults can comment about how children feel when they play: "What great fun you had playing Sorry!™"

• *Keep games fun.* Children who are too concerned about winning may not try new strategies and the game will cease to be either fun or a challenge. On the other hand, if children are playing just for fun, they may be more inclined to use new and more difficult skills. Here is an example of how even so-called educational games may lose their value if the focus is on winning.

Rajan received a computer game for his eighth birthday. It was a spelling game in which he could choose words of varying levels of difficulty or he could type in his own words. When Rajan typed in the correct spelling, he was rewarded with 10 points. After collecting 100 points, he could create a picture just for fun. After playing for several minutes, Rajan learned how to win points quickly. He simply typed in the word *a* repeatedly, then spelled it and collected 10 points.

• *Be flexible about rules.*   When children play games, it's OK to change the rules if everyone agrees.

The Cavanaugh family and a cousin were playing Aggravation™. When it got late and everyone grew tired, they agreed that each person would throw three dice, instead of one, to determine how many spaces to move. The game speeded up, and some players got as many as 18 turns in a row. Everyone laughed a lot! The cousin, however, was shocked at a family who didn't play "right," even though he enjoyed the new game.

• *Keep games challenging.*   When children have figured out all of the strategies or have become bored with the game, suggest that children change the rules to make it more complicated. Let them try their suggestions, even if you know an idea won't work—that's how children learn! What might you change? Targets for bean bags can be made smaller, more items can be added for memory games, races can be run with three legs instead of two.

Even so-called educational games may lose their value
if the focus is on winning.

How to set the context   • *Match games to children's skills.*   Tailor the Hokey Pokey to children's skills, perhaps by saying "put both arms in" or at least not being concerned about whether children really put their left or right appendage in. They will soon figure out which is left and which is right just by watching you. But be sure you face the same direction as the children or they will be totally confused! Spindly Pick-Up Sticks frustrate 3-year-olds, but usually fascinate 5-year-olds who have the fine motor skills needed to play. Children need fairly sophisticated language skills before they are ready to play Simon Says. What a great way to sharpen children's listening skills!

• *Make games available during free play.* Games are just one of many activities that may appeal to children. Now that you know the value of games, you will always want some ready for children to select. Rotate the games and offer a variety of types of games—individual, small group, large group; active and quiet; commercial, handmade, traditional. Take advantage of the weather by playing games such as Fox and Geese in the snow or playing under a shady tree in the summer.

• *Supervise children when needed.* Introduce new games by teaching children the basics of how to play, and then let them continue without interference. Competitive games can result in disagreements over rules or scorekeeping. An adult can help children figure out ways to solve their own problems—an important skill in social perspective taking. Avoid trying to settle disputes arbitrarily, because in doing so you will rob children of opportunities to solve real problems.

• *Maintain a healthy perspective on competition.* Some competition can make games more interesting, but when the purpose of games is solely to win, the games are no longer playful. Competition can be destructive if losers experience a loss of self-esteem—children need to feel good about themselves and their capabilities. Emphasize the fun of playing. Make sure some of the games available are not competitive, so that children who do not do well under pressure or who have a fragile sense of their inner resources can avoid competition. Games that depend primarily on luck, such as Ring Around the Roses and Hi-Ho! Cherry-O™, also help minimize the emphasis on winning. See Chapter 11 in Kamii and DeVries (1980) for an excellent discussion about the pros and cons of competition.

• *Find a fair way to choose teams.* Many of us remember how painful it was to always be the last person chosen for Red Rover or other team games. Eliminate this humiliating experience—select teams by birthday month (odd months on one side, even on the other) or letters of the alphabet (last names beginning with A to K on one team, L to Z on the other). Children can come up with some creative suggestions.

Always consider children's development Game playing, like other forms of play, proceeds through phases. Children first figure out how to play the game, then they practice it until the game is mastered, and finally they experiment with new rules or create new games. Here are

Competition can be destructive if losers experience a loss of self-esteem—children need to feel good about themselves and their capabilities. Emphasize the fun of playing.

some ways to make sure you choose the games best suited for the children.

- *Match the complexity of the rules with children's abilities.* The younger the child, the greater the need for games with simple rules that are few in number. First games often require color matching rather than using a die to determine moves. Follow the Leader and matching games can be tailored to almost any age group. If children seem the least bit perplexed or bored, suggest they change the rules or find another game that would be more fun for them.

- *Match the size of the group to children's abilities.* Very young children will play games alone, or perhaps with one or two other children. They are not yet ready to try strategies, but they can have a great time playing Pease Porridge Hot or Picture Dominoes. Games for young children should always keep everyone involved whenever possible. Increase the size of the group, and thus the length of time between turns, as children are able to play more cooperatively. If children wander or seem disinterested, make changes to increase their involvement.

- *Introduce complex games gradually.* Use the scaffolding process described in Chapter 3. When you learned to play Dominoes, you probably started with picture dominoes before you played with double sixes. Then you moved to double nines, and finally you progressed to double twelves. Even with complicated games, start with just a few essential rules so children can add rules as they are needed. An adult or slightly older child (one who is flexible about rules) can teach and even play the game at first until children feel comfortable on their own.

Resources about games with rules

Bogdanoff, R.F., & Dolch, E.T. (1979). Old games for young children: A link to our heritage. *Young Children, 34*(2), 37–45.

Fluegelman, A. (Ed.). (1976). *The new games book.* New York: Dolphin.

Fluegelman, A. (1981). *More new games.* New York: Dolphin.

Kamii, C., & DeVries, R. (1980). *Group games in early education: Implications of Piaget's theory.* Washington, DC: NAEYC.

Encourage behaviors related to play

Facilitate exploration   When children explore they look at, touch, smell, taste, and/or listen as a way to gain information through their senses. Although exploration is not play as we have defined it here, it usually preceeds play and should always be expected and encouraged whenever children encounter new objects, situations, or people. Children may also explore when familiar but complex toys are put away for a time and then reintroduced. Children's increased experience and maturity will enable them to discover additional properties previously overlooked.

Children need to feel safe—psychologically and physically—before they will explore. If too many objects or people are present, overstimulation may cause the child to lose focus. Give children uninterrupted time to explore and learn the possibilities for play. Remember, the box may be just as interesting as the gift inside.

Keep in mind that the world needs explorers: researchers, teachers, astronauts, chefs, community planners, clothing designers, engineers, parents—people who are curious about the world and willing to try new ways to improve the quality of life. Children take their first steps toward a lifetime of logical, scientific inquiry when they have the freedom to explore as children.

Promote children's   Children learn a great deal about language,
development   mathematics, science, social relationships, and the world in general by talking with adults and each other as they explore, play, and read or listen to stories or tapes.

• *Language and communication blossom.*   Language skills, both verbal and written, increase dramatically during the early childhood years when children are exposed to a variety of experiences. Conversation, which seems to be natural, is a cornerstone for children's learning. Interestingly, conversation includes three of the criteria for play: mutual involvement, reciprocity, and turn taking.

How you talk with children can make an enormous difference in how and what they learn. Rather than worry about correct use of speech, we should focus on what children are trying to tell us. By listening receptively, pausing to exchange turns, and using body language, we convey respect for the child—and thus make it possible to establish a warm, accepting relationship.

Light, pleasant conversations can certainly be playful as children combine ideas, make up stories, or play with their thoughts. Through conversations, children's convergent and divergent thinking is expanded. Typical questions for children might be: "If you had three wishes, what would they be?" or "What else could you do or be?" Acknowledge children's expressions ("That's certainly one way to do it.") and then encourage them to think beyond ("How else could you try?").

Children's conversations with adults and each other are a rich source of information for you. What topics or concerns are raised? How can these be incorporated either into individual conversations or perhaps field trips or new resources for the group? What clues are children giving you about their developmental levels, and how can you provide appropriate experiences based on that knowledge? Listen and watch.

By listening receptively, pausing to exchange turns, and using body language, we convey respect for the child—and thus make it possible to establish a warm, accepting relationship.

When children express anger, frustration, or sadness, language ceases to be playful. Instead, children need a secure base and a reflective listener with whom to talk. Good listening skills are the foundation for good parenting or teaching. We recommend Gordon (1970) as a resource for learning more about effective ways to talk with children. Sensitivity to children's thoughts and feelings is essential if children are to develop confidence and approach life playfully.

Resources on language and communication
Cazden, C.B. (Ed.). (1981). *Language in early childhood education* (rev. ed.). Washington, DC: NAEYC.
Gordon, T. (1970). *Parent effectiveness training*. New York: Wyden.
Zavitkovsky, D., Baker, K.R., Berlfein, J.R., & Almy, M. (1986). *Listen to the children*. Washington, DC: NAEYC.

Cognitive skills are intertwined. While talking, reading, listening, and other cognitive skills may not be classified as play on Rubin's scale, we can look at these activities in a way similar to games with rules. When they are approached with a playful attitude, the stress of learning new skills is usually reduced. Through play, children discover why they need to be able to communicate. They use different ways to learn about themselves, each other, and how things work.

Children are intrinsically motivated to learn through play. How much more meaningful it is to learn the letters in the alphabet to spell a friend's name, or to write a grocery list when playing house, or to label a block construction, than to fill in blanks on a worksheet on a topic some stranger picked! In play, skills are not isolated, but rather intertwined just as they are throughout life. Children see how economics, mathematics, and reading relate to each other through play— they write a doctor's prescription, they mark the value on tickets for a block ferry ride, they measure wood for carpentry, or they read a recipe for cooking.

Make sure children have the tools they need to develop their skills: high quality children's literature to promote an appreciation for language and art, simple-to-operate tape players to follow along with a favorite book, pads of paper and lots of implements for writing, rulers or yardsticks for measuring, plants to grow, charts to convey information children need (such as who is in charge of feeding the fish this week), labels for toy shelves, balances to compare weights—hundreds of items that will enable children to develop themes in their play.

Resources on cognitive skills
Holt, B-G. (1977). *Science with young children*. Washington, DC: NAEYC.
Kamii, C. (1982). *Number in preschool and kindergarten*. Washington, DC: NAEYC.
Lamme, L.L. (1984). *Growing up writing*. Washington, DC: Acropolis.
McCracken, J.B. (1987). *More than 1, 2, 3—The real basics of mathematics*. Washington, DC: NAEYC.
Rogers, C.S., & Wolfle, J.A. (1981). Foundations for literacy: A building blocks model. *Young Children, 36*(2), 26–32.
Schickedanz, J.A. (1986). *More than the ABCs: The early stages of reading and writing*. Washington, DC: NAEYC.

Strategies for handling play-related problems

Unoccupied behavior   At times children may wander aimlessly. If a child is frequently unoccupied, adults need to try to figure out when to help the child become more involved.

One common cause for unoccupied behavior is overstimulation. Too

In play, skills are not isolated, but rather intertwined just as they are throughout life. Make sure children have the tools they need to develop their skills.

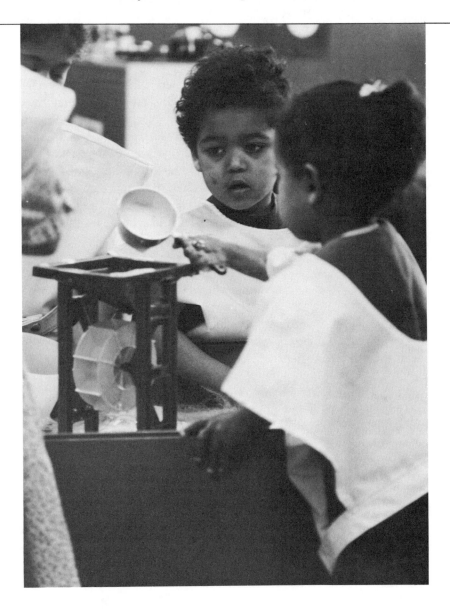

many people, too much noise, too many activities or materials may be overwhelming, especially for children who are new to the situation. Eliminate the source of the confusion (offer only a selection of the art materials, rather than everything), so children can find something to do. Or help children select from a limited number of activities ("Here's what you could do today: You could play at the water table. Or you could work on one of our new puzzles. Or you could take a book up to the loft.") Make sure your choices contain some options for quiet/noisy and active/restful activities.

Another reason children may be unoccupied is that they are bored— they are understimulated. Children long in the same program may have exhausted the possibilities of most materials. If so, you need to introduce some new items, or at least variations on the old ones. In your conversations, what topics have emerged that are of interest to these children? Now may be the time to begin a new prop box, to move the easels outdoors, or introduce an old clock to the science area. Pick up on children's ideas and use them to add variety. Take a close look at the curriculum—or at what your children usually do at home—and see how you can add some spice to children's lives.

Just looking Some children, especially those who are younger or who are new to the group, may seem content just to listen and watch other children play. While such behavior may reflect individual differences in children's activity levels, it could also mean that children need help to get involved with projects or other children's play.

When children first join a group, either at the beginning of the year or when they enter a new program, they may feel overwhelmed. What can you do? First, be sensitive and flexible; allow children time to adjust. Newcomers should be treated warmly. Ask a slightly older child to help show them around as part of their welcome. It may even help to arrange for the new child to come early on the first day, so that the other children join the new child. See Jalongo (1985) for many other strategies to help children adjust to moving.

Children who have been in the group for some time and who seem to be unpopular may need additional attention to help them develop their social skills. Roopnarine and Honig (1985) suggest that we take steps to enhance these children's self-esteem; that we encourage them to participate in small groups at first; and that we use puppets, reverse role playing, or books to demonstrate other interaction styles.

Resources for handling play-related problems
Jalongo, M.R. (1985). When young children move. *Young Children, 40*(6), 51–57.
Roopnarine, J.L., & Honig, A.S. (1985). Research in review. The unpopular child. *Young Children, 40*(6), 59–64.

Transitions

The times you and the children spend preparing for, setting up, cleaning up, or changing from one activity to another are known as transitions. Throughout this book, we have emphasized the need for children to have ample time to develop their play themes, to work through their ideas, and to complete games. Therefore, it is logical that there should be as few transitions as possible during the day. Some, obviously, are essential.

Children are often reluctant to end their play, especially when someone else asks them to do so. If you prepare children in advance— "It's just 5 minutes until cleanup time"—they will be much more likely to be ready to stop than if they suddenly must interrupt their play. Sometimes adult supervision and participation is necessary. Remember how the pirates eagerly helped to store the gold nuggets? Sometimes a large project, such as an intricate block structure, will need to be saved rather than destroyed. Flexibility is necessary to keep transitions smooth for everyone.

In group programs, transition times are when the most adults are needed to join in, to remind children about the next pleasant activity, and to reassure children that the materials or equipment will be there again another day. For some excellent ideas about how to ease children from one activity to another, we suggest you read the very practical article by Alger (1984).

Resource on transitions
Alger, H.A. (1984). Transitions: Alternatives to manipulative management techniques. *Young Children, 39*(6), 16–25.

Aggression

Whenever groups of children play, you can expect to encounter children who are angry or upset and who hit, kick, bite, or threaten. Their targets may be other children, the adults, or the toys. This type of aggressive behavior is not rough-and-tumble play, and it is of great concern to parents and teachers.

Why are children aggressive? Sometimes they come from authoritarian environments in which they are highly controlled and have few choices—the result is frustration that leads to aggression. The environment can also be the problem if the expectations for children's behavior are not appropriate—children should not have to wait in line for long periods, for example, while everyone else gets their coats on to go outdoors.

Or it may be that there is not enough space or appropriate places for children to play: Perhaps there are too few toys and activities for the number of children, or the toys and activities are not appropriate for the children's developmental levels and interests. Sometimes children younger than 3 are expected to share, when they are not yet developmentally ready to do so, or preschool children are required to sit quietly at tables doing worksheets. No wonder aggression finds its way into children's lives!

The first place to look for some solutions to aggressive behavior, then, is the environment, in programs or in your home:

• Are children treated with respect? For example, children need to feel secure and loved. "Randy, people are not for hitting. I know you are angry. Let's talk about what happened." Children who feel good about themselves and others are less likely to be aggressive.

• Are children guided to learn to control themselves (rather than just expected to follow your orders)? Notice when they are good. "Josh, you must feel so proud that you shared your blocks with Cara." Offer positive alternatives. Establish fair rules. Help children see how their behavior affects others.

• Are the activities and materials sufficient and appropriate? Be sure several of the most popular toys are available for infants and toddlers. Match the curriculum to the children's abilities and interests. Arrange the schedule and the room to allow enough time and space for play.

• Are children given opportunites to resolve their own disagreements by using words? "Jessica, it looks like you would like to play with the bucket Virat has. Instead of grabbing it from him, what can you say that might encourage him to share with you?" Do not arbitrarily resolve disagreements.

Leading children toward self-discipline is not an easy task, but there are some techniques that are much more effective than punishment. We urge you to learn more about appropriate techniques for working with children, so that their play, and their entire lives, will be enriched.

Resources on discipline

Gartrell, D. (1987). Punishment or guidance? *Young Children, 42*(3), 55–61.

Honig, A.S. (1985). *Love and learn: Discipline for young children.* Washington, DC: NAEYC.

NAEYC. (1986). *Helping children learn self-control: A guide to discipline.* Washington, DC: Author.

Stone, J.G. (1978). *A guide to discipline.* Washington, DC: NAEYC.

Weber-Schwartz, N. (1987). Patience or understanding? *Young Children, 42*(3), 52–54.

Summary

Until you read this book, you may have thought that children's play was simple. You may have thought that adults had very little to do with children's play, except perhaps to buy some toys. Instead, we have seen how complicated children's play really is, how crucial play is to healthy development, and how important it is for us to observe and respond appropriately to children's play. Only when we are well informed about the value of play, and know how to foster productive play, can we take steps to help children get the most from their favorite activities. Here are some questions that will help you make good decisions about how to guide children's play.

- Are children happy, with twinkles in their eyes?

- What emotions are being expressed?

- What type of play is it: practice, symbolic, or games with rules?

- How sophisticated is the play and the symbolism involved?

- What is the level of social involvement?

- What knowledge about the world do the children's actions and comments reflect?

- What are the children's interests?

- Does the play focus on the process rather than the product?

- How does the play further your goals for children?

References

A

Alger, H. A. (1984). Transitions: Alternatives to manipulative management techniques. *Young Children, 39* (6), 16–25.

Athey, I. (1984). Contributions of play to development. In T. D. Yawkey & A. D. Pellegrini (Eds.), *Child's play: Developmental and applied* (pp. 9–27). Hillsdale, NJ: Erlbaum.

Atkinson, J., Braddick, O., & Moar, K. (1977). Contrast sensitivity of the human infant for moving and static patterns. *Vision Research, 17,* 1045–1047.

B

Bakeman, R., & Adamson, L. B. (1984). Coordinating attention to people and objects in mother-infant and peer-infant interaction. *Child Development, 55,* 1278–1289.

Bakeman, R. E., & Brown, J. (1977). Behavior dialogues: An approach to the assessment of mother-infant interaction. *Child Development, 48,* 195–203.

Bakeman, R., & Brownlee, J. R. (1980). The strategic use of parallel play: A sequential analysis. *Child Development, 51,* 873–878.

Banks, M. S., & Salapatek, P. (1983). Infant visual perception. In M. M. Haith & J. J. Campos (Eds.), P. H. Mussen (Series Ed.), *Handbook of child psychology: Vol. 2. Infancy and developmental psychobiology* (pp. 435–571). New York: Wiley.

Barnes, K. E. (1971). Preschool play norms: A replication. *Developmental Psychology, 5,* 99–103.

Bateson, G. (1956). The message "This is play." In B. Schaffner (Ed.), *Group processes* (pp. 145–151). New York: Josiah Macy.

Becker, J. M. T. (1977). A learning analysis of the development of peer-oriented behavior in nine-month-old infants. *Developmental Psychology, 13,* 481–491.

Beckwith, L. (1985). Parent-child interaction and social-emotional development. In C. C. Brown & A. W. Gottfried (Eds.), *Play interactions: The role of toys and parental involvement in children's development* (pp. 152–159). Skillman, NJ: Johnson & Johnson.

Beller, E. K., Zimmie, J., & Aiken, L. (1971). Levels of play in different nursery settings. *International Congress of Applied Psychology,* Liege, Belgium.

Belsky, J., Goode, M. K., & Most, R. K. (1980). Maternal stimulation and infant exploratory competence: Cross-sectional, correlational, and experimental analyses. *Child Development, 51,* 1163–1178.

Belsky, J., & Most, R. K. (1981). From exploration to play: A cross-sectional study of infant free play behavior. *Developmental Psychology, 17,* 630–639.

Bentovim, A. (1977). The role of play in psychotherapeutic work with children and their families. In B. Tizard & D. Harvey (Eds.), *Biology of play* (pp. 185–198). Philadelphia: Lippincott.

Berlyne, D. (1966). Curiosity and exploration. *Science, 153*, 25–33.

Berlyne, D. (1969). Laughter, humor and play. In G. Lindzey & E. Aronson (Eds.), *The handbook of social psychology* (Vol. 3) (pp. 795–852). Reading, MA: Addison-Wesley.

Bolig, R. (1984). Play in hospital. In T. D. Yawkey & A. D. Pellegrini (Eds.), *Child's play: Developmental and applied* (pp. 323–345). Hillsdale, NJ: Erlbaum.

Bradley, R. H. (1985). Play materials and intellectual development. In C. C. Brown & A. W. Gottfried (Eds.), *Play interactions: The role of toys and parental involvement in children's development* (pp. 129–142). Skillman, NJ: Johnson & Johnson.

Brainerd, C. J. (1982). Effects of group and individualized dramatic play training on cognitive development. In D. J. Pepler & K. H. Rubin (Eds.), *The play of children: Current theory and research* (pp. 114–129). Basel, Switzerland: Karger.

Bretherton, I. (1984). Representing the social world in symbolic play: Reality and fantasy. In I. Bretherton (Ed.), *Symbolic play: The development of social understanding* (pp. 1–41). New York: Academic.

Bretherton, I. (1985). Pretense: Practicing and playing with social understanding. In C. C. Brown & A. W. Gottfried (Eds.), *Play interactions: The role of toys and parental involvement in children's development* (pp. 69–79). Skillman, NJ: Johnson & Johnson.

Bronson, W. C. (1975). Developments in behavior with age mates during the second year of life. In M. Lewis & L. A. Rosenblum (Eds.), *Friendship and peer relations* (pp. 131–152). New York: Wiley.

Brownell, C. A. (1982). Peer interaction among toddler aged children: Effects of age and social context on interactional competence and behavior roles. *Dissertation Abstracts International, 43*, 2727B. (University Microfilms No. DA8301909)

Bruner, J. S. (1972). The nature and uses of immaturity. *American Psychologist, 27*, 687–708.

Bruner, J. S., & Sherwood, V. (1976). Peekaboo and the learning of rule structures. In J. S. Bruner, A. Jolly, & K. Sylva (Eds.), *Play—Its role in development and evolution* (pp. 277–285). New York: Basic.

Burns, S. M., & Brainerd, C. J. (1979). Effects of constructive and dramatic play on perspective-taking in very young children. *Developmental Psychology, 15*, 512–521.

C

Caldwell, B. M. (1985). Parent-child play: A playful evaluation. In C. C. Brown & A. W. Gottfried (Eds.), *Play interactions: The role of toys and parental involvement in children's development* (pp. 167–178). Skillman, NJ: Johnson & Johnson.

Campbell, F. (1972). Preschool behavior study. *Architectural Psychology Newsletter, 3*(1), 4.

Campbell, S. P., & Frost, J. L. (1978, August). *The effects of playground type on the cognitive and social play behaviors of grade two children.* Paper presented at the Seventh World Congress of the International Playground Association, Ottawa, Ontario, Canada.

Carpenter, C. (1979, March). *Relation of children's sex-typed behavior to classroom and activity structure.* Paper presented at the Biennial Meeting of the Society for Research in Child Development, San Francisco.

Cazden, C. (1974). Play with language and metalinguistic awareness: One dimension of language experience. *The Urban Review, 7*, 28–39.

Cheyne, J. A., & Rubin, K. H. (1983). Play precursors of problem-solving in preschoolers. *Developmental Psychology, 19*, 577–584.

Cicchetti, D. (1985). Caregiver-infant interaction: The study of maltreated infants. In C. C. Brown & A. W. Gottfried (Eds.), *Play interactions: The role of toys and parental involvement in children's development* (pp. 107–113). Skillman, NJ: Johnson & Johnson.

Collard, R. R. (1979). Exploration and play. In B. Sutton-Smith (Ed.), *Play and learning* (pp. 45–68). New York: Gardner.

Confer, C. (1984). Alleviating aggressive behaviors using therapy and play objects in the psychoanalytic mainstream. In T. D. Yawkey & A. D. Pellegrini (Eds.), *Child's play and play therapy* (pp. 105–115). Lancaster, PA: Technomic.

Connell, J. P. (1985). A new multidimensional measure of children's perceptions of control. *Child Development, 56*, 1018–1041.

Connolly, J. (1980). *The relationship between social pretend play and social competence in preschoolers: Correlational and experimental studies.* Unpublished doctoral dissertation, Concordia University, Montreal, Canada.

Csikszentmihalyi, M. (1975). *Beyond boredom and anxiety.* San Francisco: Jossey-Bass.

Csikszentmihalyi, M. (1979). The concept of flow. In B. Sutton-Smith (Ed.), *Play and learning* (pp. 257–274). New York: Gardner.

Curry, N. E., & Arnaud, S. H. (1984). Play in developmental preschool settings. In T. D. Yawkey & A. D. Pellegrini (Eds.), *Child's play: Developmental and applied* (pp. 273– 290). Hillsdale, NJ: Erlbaum.

D

Dansky, J. L. (1980a). Make-believe: A mediator of the relationship between play and associative fluency. *Child Development, 51*, 576–579.

Dansky, J. L. (1980b). Cognitive consequences of sociodramatic play and exploration training for economically disadvantaged preschoolers. *Journal of Child Psychology and Psychiatry, 20*, 47–58.

Dansky, J. L., & Silverman, I. W. (1973). Effects of play on associative fluency in preschool-aged children. *Developmental Psychology, 9*, 38–43.

Dansky, J. L., & Silverman, I .W. (1975). Play: A general facilitator of associative fluency. *Developmental Psychology, 11*, 104.

Darvill, D. (1982). Ecological influences on children's play: Issues and approaches. In D. J. Pepler & K. H. Rubin (Eds.), *The play of children: Current theory and research* (pp. 143–153). Basel, Switzerland: Karger.

DeLoache, J. S., Sugarman, S., & Brown, A. L. (1985). The development of error correction strategies in young children's manipulative play. *Child Development, 56*, 928–939.

DeStefano, C. T., & Muller, E. (1980). *Environmental determinants of peer social activity in 18 month old males.* Unpublished manuscript, Boston University.

Diantoniis, J. M., & Yawkey, T. D. (1984). Child's play as therapy. In T. D. Yawkey & A. D. Pellegrini (Eds.), *Child's play and play therapy* (pp. 79–84). Lancaster, PA: Technomic.

Doyle, A., Connolly, J., & Rivest, L. (1980). The effects of playmate familiarity on the social interactions of young children. *Child Development, 51*, 217–223.

Dreyer, A. S., & Rigler, D. (1969). Cognitive performance in Montessori and nursery school children. *Journal of Educational Research, 62*, 411–416.

Dunn, J. (1985). Pretend play in the family. In C. C. Brown & A. W. Gottfried (Eds.), *Play interactions: The role of toys and parental involvement in children's development* (pp. 79–88). Skillman, NJ: Johnson & Johnson.

E

Eckerman, C. O., & Whatley, J. L. (1977). Toys and social interaction between infant peers. *Child Development, 48*, 1645–1656.

Eifermann, R. R. (1971). Social play in childhood. In R. E. Herron & B. Sutton-Smith (Eds.), *Child's play* (pp. 270–297). New York: Wiley.

Elder, J., & Pederson, D. (1978). Preschool children's use of objects in symbolic play. *Child Development, 49*, 500–504.

Elkind, D. (1986). Formal education and early childhood education: An essential difference. *Phi Delta Kappan, 67*, 631–636.

Ellis, M. (1973). *Why people play*. Englewood Cliffs, NJ: Prentice-Hall.

Ellis, M. (1979). The complexity of objects and peers. In B. Sutton-Smith (Ed.), *Play and learning* (pp. 157–174). New York: Gardner.

Erikson, E. H. (1963). *Childhood and society* (2nd ed.). New York: Norton.

Erikson, E. H. (1977). *Toys and reasons*. New York: Norton.

F

Fagan, R. (1984). Play and behavioral flexibility. In P. K. Smith (Ed.), *Play in animals and humans* (pp. 159–173). New York: Blackwell.

Fantz, R. L. (1961). The origin of form perception. *Scientific American, 204*(5), 66–72.

Farson, R. (1971). Praise reappraised. In R. Strom (Ed.), *Learning process* (pp. 25–32). Englewood Cliffs, NJ: Prentice-Hall.

Fein, G. G. (1975). A transformational analysis of pretending. *Developmental Psychology, 11*, 291–296.

Fein, G. G. (1979). Play with actions and objects. In B. Sutton-Smith (Ed.), *Play and learning* (pp. 69–82). New York: Gardner.

Fein, G. G. (1981a). Pretend play in childhood: An integrative review. *Child Development, 52*, 1095–1118.

Fein, G. G. (1981b). The physical environment: Stimulation or evocation. In R. M. Lerner & N. A. Busch-Rossnagel (Eds.), *Individuals as producers of their development: A life-span perspective* (pp. 257–279). New York: Academic.

Fein, G. G. (1985). The affective psychology of play. In C. C. Brown & A. W. Gottfried (Eds.), *Play interactions: The role of toys and parental involvement in children's development* (pp. 19–28). Skillman, NJ: Johnson & Johnson.

Fein, G. G., & Apfel, N. (1979). Some preliminary observations on knowing and pretending. In N. Smith & M. Franklin (Eds.), *Symbolic functioning in childhood* (pp. 87–100). Hillsdale, NJ: Erlbaum.

Feitelson, D. (1977). Cross-cultural studies of representational play. In B. Tizard & D. Harvey (Eds.), *Biology of play* (pp. 6–14). Philadelphia: Lippincott.

Feitelson, D., & Ross, G. S. (1973). The neglected factor—play. *Human Development*, *16*, 202–223.

Fenson, L. (1984). Developmental trends for action and speech in pretend play. In I. Bretherton (Ed.), *Symbolic play: The development of social understanding* (pp. 249–270). New York: Academic.

Fenson, L. (1985). The developmental progression of exploration and play. In C. C. Brown & A. W. Gottfried (Eds.), *Play interactions: The role of toys and parental involvement in children's development* (pp. 31–38). Skillman, NJ: Johnson & Johnson.

Fenson, L., Kagan, J., Kearsley, R. B., & Zelazo, P. R. (1976). The developmental progression of manipulative play in the first two years. *Child Development*, *47*, 232–236.

Fenson, L., & Ramsay, D. S. (1980). Decentration and integration of child's play in the second year. *Child Development*, *51*, 171–178.

Fenson, L., & Ramsay, D. S. (1981). Effects of modeling action sequences on the play of twelve-, fifteen-, and nineteen-month-old children. *Child Development*, *52*, 1028–1036.

Forys, S. K. S., & McCune-Nicolich, L. (1984). Shared pretend: Socio-dramatic play at 3 years of age. In I. Bretherton (Ed.), *Symbolic play: The development of social understanding* (pp. 159-191). New York: Academic.

Freyberg, J. (1973). Increasing the imaginative play of urban disadvantaged kindergarten children through systematic training. In J. L. Singer (Ed.), *The child's world of make-believe* (pp. 129-154). New York: Academic.

G

Garvey, C. (1977). *Play*. Cambridge, MA: Harvard University Press.

Garvey, C. (1979). Communication controls in social play. In B. Sutton-Smith (Ed.), *Play and learning* (pp. 109–125). New York: Gardner.

Giffin, H. (1984). The coordination of meaning in the creation of a shared make-believe reality. In I. Bretherton (Ed.), *Symbolic play: The development of social understanding* (pp. 73–100). New York: Academic.

Glickman, C. D. (1984). Play in the public school settings: A philosophical question. In T. D. Yawkey & A. D. Pellegrini (Eds.), *Child's play: Developmental and applied* (pp. 255–271). Hillsdale, NJ: Erlbaum.

Gordon, T. (1970). *Parent effectiveness training*. New York: Wyden.

Gottfried, A. E. (1985). Intrinsic motivation for play. In C. C. Brown & A. W. Gottfried (Eds.). *Play interactions: The role of toys and parental involvement in children's development* (pp. 45–52). Skillman, NJ: Johnson & Johnson.

Gottfried, A. W. (1985a). Introduction. In C. C. Brown & A. W. Gottfried (Eds.), *Play interactions: The role of toys and parental involvement in children's development* (pp. xvii–xx). Skillman, NJ: Johnson & Johnson.

Gottfried, A. W. (1985b). The relationships of play materials and parental involvement to young children's development. In C. C. Brown & A. W. Gottfried (Eds.), *Play interactions: The role of toys and parental involvement in children's development* (pp. 181–185). Skillman, NJ: Johnson & Johnson.

Gottfried, A. W., & Gottfried, A. E. (1984). Home environment and cognitive development in young children of middle-socio-economic-status families. In A. W.

Gottfried (Ed.), *Home environment and early cognitive development: Longitudinal research* (pp. 57–115). New York: Academic.

Gottlieb, G. (1983). The psychobiological approach to developmental issues. In M. M. Haith and J. J. Campos (Eds.), P. H. Mussen (Series Ed.), *Handbook of child psychology: Vol. 2. Infancy and developmental psychobiology* (pp. 1–26). New York: Wiley.

Guerney, L. F. (1984). Play therapy in counseling settings. In T. D. Yawkey & A. D. Pellegrini (Eds.), *Child's play: Developmental and applied* (pp. 291–321). Hillsdale, NJ: Erlbaum.

H

Harper, L. V., & Huie, K. S. (1985). The effects of prior group experience, age, and familiarity on the quality and organization of preschoolers' social relationships. *Child Development, 56*, 704–717.

Harris, P. L. (1983). Infant cognition. In M. M. Haith & J. J. Campos (Eds.), P. H. Mussen (Series Ed.), *Handbook of child psychology: Vol. 2. Infancy and developmental psychobiology* (pp. 689–782). New York: Wiley.

Harter, S. (1978). Effectance motivation reconsidered: Toward a developmental model. *Human Development, 21*, 34–64.

Harter, S. (1981). A model of mastery motivation in children: Individual differences and developmental change. In W. A. Collins (Ed.), *Minnesota symposium on child psychology* (Vol. 14) (pp. 215–255). Hillsdale, NJ: Erlbaum.

Harter, S. (1983) Developmental perspectives on the self-system. In M. Hetherington (Ed.), P. H. Mussen (Series Ed.), *Handbook of child psychology: Vol. 4. Socialization, personality, and social development* (pp. 275–385). New York: Wiley.

Hartup, W. W. (1983). Peer relations. In E. M. Hetherington (Ed.), P. H. Mussen (Series Ed.), *Handbook of child psychology: Vol. 4. Socialization, personality and social development* (pp. 103–196). New York: Wiley.

Hay, D. F., Nash, A., & Pedersen, J. (1983). Interaction between six-month-old peers. *Child Development, 54*, 557–562.

Hay, D. F., Ross, H. S., & Goldman, B. D. (1979). Social games in infancy. In B. Sutton-Smith (Ed.), *Play and learning* (pp. 83–107). New York: Gardner.

Hetherington, E. M., Cox, M., & Cox, R. (1979). Play and social interaction in children following divorce. *Journal of Social Issues, 35*(4), 26–49.

Hodapp, R. M., Goldfield, E. C., & Boyatzis, C. J. (1984). The use of effectiveness of maternal scaffolding in mother-infant games. *Child Development, 55*, 772–781.

Hole, G. J., & Einon, D. F. (1984). Play in rodents. In P. K. Smith (Ed.), *Play in animals and humans* (pp. 95–117). New York: Blackwell.

Hunt, J. M. (1961). *Intelligence and experience*. New York: The Ronald Press.

Hurlock, E. B. (1971). Experimental investigations of childhood play. In R. E. Herron & B. Sutton-Smith (Eds.), *Child's play* (pp. 51–70). New York: Wiley.

Huston-Stein, A., Friedrich-Cofer, L., & Susman, E. J. (1977). The relation of classroom structures to social behavior, imaginative play, and self-regulation of economically disadvantaged children. *Child Development, 48*, 908–916.

Hutt, C. (1976). Exploration and play in children. In J. S. Bruner, A. Jolly, & K. Sylva (Eds.), *Play—Its role in development and evolution* (pp. 202–215). New York: Basic.

Hutt, C. (1979). Exploration and play. In B. Sutton-Smith (Ed.), *Play and learning* (pp. 175–194). New York: Gardner.

Hutt, C., & Bhavnani, R. (1976). Predictions from play. In J. S. Bruner, A. Jolly, & K. Sylva (Eds.), *Play—Its role in development and evolution* (pp. 216–219). New York: Basic.

Hutt, C., & Vaizey, M. J. (1966). Differential effects of group density on social behavior. *Nature, 209*, 1371–1372.

J

Jackowitz, E. R., & Watson, M. W. (1980). The development of object transformations in early pretend play. *Developmental Psychology, 16*, 543–549.

Jacobson, J. L. (1981). The role of inanimate objects in early peer interaction. *Child Development, 52*, 618–626.

Jalongo, M.R. (1985). When young children move. *Young Children, 40* (6), 51–57.

Jeffers, V. W., & Lore, R. K. (1979). Let's play at my house: Effects of the home environment on social behavior of children. *Child Development, 50*, 837–841.

Jeffree, D., & McConkey, R. (1976). An observation scheme for recording children's imaginative doll play. *Journal of Child Psychology and Psychiatry, 17*, 189–197.

Jennings, K. D., Harmon, R. S., Morgan, G. A., Gaiter, J. L., & Yarrow, L. J. (1979). Exploratory play as an index of mastery motivation: Relationships to persistence, cognitive functioning, and environmental measures. *Developmental Psychology, 15*, 386–394.

Johnson, J. E. (1976). Relations of divergent thinking and intelligence test scores with social and nonsocial make-believe play of preschool children. *Child Development, 47*, 1200–1203.

Johnson, J. E., & Ershler, J. (1981). Developmental trends in preschool play as a function of classroom setting and child gender. *Child Development, 52*, 995–1004.

Johnson, J. E., & Ershler, J. (1982). Curricular effects on the play of preschoolers. In D. J. Pepler & K. H. Rubin (Eds.), *The play of children: Current theory and research* (pp. 130–143). Basel, Switzerland: Karger.

Johnson, J. E., Ershler, J., & Bell, C. (1980). Play behavior in a discovery-based and a formal education preschool program. *Child Development, 51*, 271–274.

Johnson, M. W. (1935). The effect on behavior of variation in the amount of play equipment. *Child Development, 6*, 56–68.

K

Kalveboer, A. F. (1977). Measurement of play: Clinical applications. In B. Tizard & D. Harvey (Eds.), *Biology of play* (p. 100–122). Philadelphia: Lippincott.

Kamii, C. (1982). *Number in preschool and kindergarten: Educational implications of Piaget's theory.* Washington, DC: NAEYC.

Kamii, C., & DeVries, R. (1980). *Group games in early education: Implications of Piaget's theory.* Washington, DC: NAEYC.

Kee, D. W. (1985). Computer play. In C. C. Brown & A. W. Gottfried (Eds.), *Play interactions: The role of toys and parental involvement in children's development* (pp. 53–60). Skillman, NJ: Johnson & Johnson.

Kirshenblatt-Gimblet, B. (Ed.). (1976). *Speech play.* Philadelphia: University of Pennsylvania Press.

Kogan, N. (1983). Stylistic variation in childhood and adolescence: Creativity, metaphor and cognitive styles. In J. H. Flavell & E. Markman (Eds.), P. H. Mussen (Series Ed.), *Handbook of child psychology: Vol. 3. Cognitive development* (pp. 630–706). New York: Wiley.

Krasnor, L. R., & Pepler, D. J. (1980). The study of children's play: Some suggested future directions. In K. H. Rubin (Ed.), *New directions in child development: Children's play* (pp. 85–95). San Francisco: Jossey-Bass.

Kreye, M. (1984). Conceptual organization in the play of preschool children: Effects of meaning, context, and mother-child interaction. In I. Bretherton (Ed.), *Symbolic play: The development of social understanding* (pp. 299–336). New York: Academic.

Kritchevsky, S., & Prescott, E. (1977). *Planning environments for young children: Physical space* (rev. ed.). Washington, DC: NAEYC.

L

Leeper, M. R., Greene, P., & Nisbett, R. E. (1973). Undermining children's intrinsic interest with extrinsic rewards: A test of the "overjustification" hypothesis. *Journal of Personality and Social Psychology, 28*, 129–137.

Levenstein, P. (1985). Mothers' interactive behavior in play sessions and children's educational achievement. In C. C. Brown and A. W. Gottfried (Eds.), *Play interactions: The role of toys and parental involvement in children's development* (pp. 160–165). Skillman, NJ: Johnson & Johnson.

Levy, J. (1978). *Play behavior*. New York: Wiley.

Lewin, K.L. (1935). *A dynamic theory of personality: Selected papers of Kurt Lewin*. New York: McGraw-Hill.

Li, A. K. (1978). Effects at play on novel responses in kindergarten children. *The Alberta Journal of Educational Research, 24*, 31–36.

Lieberman, J. N. (1965). Playfulness and divergent thinking: An investigation of their relationship at the kindergarten level. *The Journal of Genetic Psychology, 107*, 219–224.

Lindquist, I., Lind, J., & Harvey, D. (1977). Play in hospital. In B. Tizard & D. Harvey (Eds.), *Biology of play* (pp. 160–169). Philadelphia: Lippincott.

M

MacTurk, R. H., Vietze, P. M., McCarthy, M. E., McQuiston, S., & Yarrow, L. (1985). The organization of exploratory behavior in Down syndrome and nondelayed infants. *Child Development, 56*, 573–581.

Mann, B. L. (1984). Fill and dump play: Mastery of handling skills and object permanence. In T. D. Yawkey & A. D. Pellegrini (Eds.), *Child's play and play therapy* (pp. 59–76). Lancaster, PA: Technomic.

Martin, P. C. (1984). The study of play in mammals. In P. K. Smith (Ed.), *Play in animals and humans* (pp. 71–94). New York: Blackwell.

Matas, L., Arend, R. A., & Sroufe, L. A. (1978). Continuity of adaptation in the second year: The relationship between quality of attachment and later competence. *Child Development, 49*, 547–556.

Matthews, W. S. (1977). Modes of transformation in the initiation of fantasy play. *Developmental Psychology, 13*, 212–216.

Matthews, W. S. (1978, March). *Interruptions of fantasy play: A matter of breaking frame*. Paper presented at the meeting of the Eastern Psychological Association, Washington, DC.

Matthews, W. S., Beebe, S., & Bopp, W. (1980). Spatial perspective-taking and pretend play. *Perceptual and Motor Skills*, *51*, 49–50.

Mauer, D., & Salapatek, P. (1976). Developmental changes in the scanning of faces by young infants. *Child Development*, *47*, 523–527.

McCall, R. B. (1974). Exploratory manipulation and play in the human infant. *Monographs of the Society for Research in Child Development*, *39* (2, Serial No. 155).

McCall, R. B. (1979). Stages in play development between zero and two years of age. In B. Sutton-Smith (Ed.), *Play and learning* (pp. 35–44). New York: Gardner.

McCune, L. (1985). Play-language relationships and symbolic development. In C. C. Brown and A. W. Gottfried (Eds.), *Play interactions: The role of toys and parental involvement in children's development* (pp. 38–45). Skillman, NJ: Johnson & Johnson.

McCune-Nicolich, L., & Bruskin, C. (1982). Combinatorial competency in symbolic play and language. In D. J. Pepler & K. H. Rubin (Eds.), *The play of children: Current theory and research* (pp. 30–45). Basel, Switzerland: Karger.

McGrew, W. C. (1972). *An ethological study of children's behavior*. London: Academic.

McLoyd, V. C. (1983). The effects of the structure of play objects on the pretend play of low-income preschool children. *Child Development*, *54*, 626–635.

McLoyd, V. C. (1985). Social class and pretend play. In C. C. Brown & A. W. Gottfried (Eds.), *Play interactions: The role of toys and parental involvement in children's development* (pp. 96–104). Skillman, NJ: Johnson & Johnson.

Meltzoff, A. N. (1985). Immediate and deferred imitation in fourteen- and twenty-four-month-old infants. *Child Development*, *56*, 62–72.

Miller, L. B., & Dyer, J. L. (1975). Four preschool programs: Their dimensions and effects. *Monographs of the Society for Research in Child Development*, *40*, (5–6, Serial No. 162).

Miller, P., & Garvey, C. (1984). Mother-baby role play: Its origins in social support. In I. Bretherton (Ed.), *Symbolic play: The development of social understanding* (pp. 101–130). New York: Academic.

Miller, T. J. (1984). Therapist-child relations in play therapy. In T. D. Yawkey & A. D. Pellegrini (Eds.), *Child's play and play therapy* (pp. 85–103). Lancaster, PA: Technomic.

Mogford, K. (1977). The play of handicapped children. In B. Tizard & D. Harvey (Eds.), *Biology of play* (pp. 170–184). Philadelphia: Lippincott.

Moore, N. V., Evertson, C. M., & Brophy, J. E. (1974). Solitary play: Some functional reconsiderations. *Developmental Psychology*, *10*, 830–834.

Moran, J. D., Sawyers, J. K., Fu, V. R., & Milgram, R. M. (1984). Predicting imaginative play in preschool children. *Gifted Child Quarterly*, *28*, 92–94.

Moran, J. D., Sawyers, J. K., & Moore, A. J. (in press). The effects of structure in instructions and materials on preschoolers' creativity. *Acta Paedologica*.

Mueller, E., & Brenner, J. (1977). The origins of social skills and interaction among playgroup toddlers. *Child Development*, *48*, 854–861.

Mueller, E., & Lucas, T. (1975). A developmental analysis of peer interaction among toddlers. In M. Lewis & L. Rosenblum (Eds.), *Friendship and peer relations*. New York: Wiley.

N

Nahme-Huang, L., Singer, D. G., Singer, J. L., & Wheaton, A. (1977). Imaginative play and perceptual-motor intervention methods with emotionally-disturbed hospitalized children: An evaluation study. *American Journal of Orthopsychiatry, 47*, 238–249.

Nelson, K., & Seidman, S. (1984). Playing with scripts. In I. Bretherton (Ed.), *Symbolic play: The development of social understanding* (pp. 45–71). New York: Academic.

Nicolich, L. (1977). Beyond sensori-motor intelligence: Assessment of symbolic maturity through analysis of pretend play. *Merrill-Palmer Quarterly, 23*, 89–99.

Nunnally, J. C., & Lemond, L. C. (1973). Exploratory behavior and human development. In H. Reese (Ed.), *Advances in child development and behavior* (Vol. 8) (pp. 60–106). New York: Academic.

O

Olszewski, P., & Fuson, K. C. (1982). Verbally expressed fantasy play of preschoolers as a function of toy structure, *Developmental Psychology, 18*, 57–61.

Overton, W. F., & Jackson, J. P. (1973). The representation of imagined objects in action sequence: A developmental study. *Child Development, 44*, 309–314.

P

Parten, M. B. (1932). Social participation among preschool children. *Journal of Abnormal Psychology, 27*, 243–269.

Pellegrini, A. D. (1980). The relationships between kindergartners' play and reading, writing and language achievement. *Psychology in the School, 17*, 530–535.

Pellegrini, A. D. (1984). Children's play and language: Infancy through early childhood. In T. D. Yawkey & A. D. Pellegrini (Eds.), *Child's play and play therapy* (pp. 45–58). Lancaster, PA: Technomic.

Pellegrini, A. D., & Galda, L. (1982). The effects of thematic fantasy play training on the development of children's story comprehension. *American Education Research Journal, 19*, 443–452.

Pepler, D. J., & Ross, H. S. (1981). The effects of play on convergent and divergent problem-solving. *Child Development, 52*, 1202–1210.

Phyfe-Perkins, E. (1980). Children's behavior in preschool settings—Review of research concerning the influence of the physical environment. In L. G. Katz (Ed.), *Current topics in early childhood education* (Vol. 3) (pp. 91–125). Norwood, NJ: Ablex.

Piaget, J. (1962). *Play, dreams, and imitation in childhood* (C. Gattegno & F. M. Hodgson, Trans.). New York: Norton. (Original work published 1951)

Piaget, J. (1963). *The origins of intelligence in children* (M. Cook, Trans.). New York: Norton.

Piaget, J. (1965). *The moral judgment of the child* (M. Gabain, Trans.). New York: Free Press. (Original work published 1932)

Piaget, J. (1970). Piaget's theory. (G. Gellerier & J. Langer, Trans.) In P. H. Mussen (Ed.), *Carmichael's manual of child psychology* (3rd ed.) (Vol. 1) (pp. 703–732). New York: Wiley.

Porrata-Doria, Z. (1984). Play: The father's primary way of contributing to the young child's development. In T. D. Yawkey & A. D. Pellegrini (Eds.), *Child's play and play therapy* (pp. 147–155). Lancaster, PA: Technomic.

Power, T. G. (1985). Mother- and father-infant play: A developmental analysis. *Child Development, 56*, 1514–1524.

Power, T. G., & Parke, R. D. (1983). Patterns of mother and father play with their 8-month-old infants: A multiple analyses approach. *Infant Behavior and Development, 6*, 453–459.

Prescott, E., Jones, E., & Kritchevsky, S. (1967). *Group day care as a child rearing environment: An observational study of day care programs*. Pasadena, CA: Pacific Oaks College. (ERIC Document Reproduction Service No. ED 024 453)

Pulaski, M. A. S. (1970). Play as a function of toy structure and fantasy predisposition. *Child Development, 41*, 531–537.

Q

Qiltich, H. R., & Risley, T. (1973). The effects of play materials on social play. *Journal of Applied Behavioral Analysis, 6*, 575–578.

Quinn, J. M., & Rubin, K. H. (1984). The play of handicapped children. In T. D. Yawkey & A. D. Pellegrini (Eds.), *Child's play: Developmental and applied* (pp. 63–80). Hillsdale, NJ: Erlbaum.

R

Ramey, C. T., Finklestein, N. W., & O'Brien, C. (1976). Toys and infant behavior in the first year of life. *Journal of Genetic Psychology, 129*, 341–342.

Roopnarine, J. L., & Honig, A. S. (1985). Research in review. The unpopular child. *Young Children, 40*(6), 59–64.

Roper, R., & Hinde, R. A. (1978). Social behavior in a play group: Consistency and complexity. *Child Development, 49*, 570–579.

Rosen, C. E. (1974). The effects of sociodramatic play on problem-solving behavior among culturally disadvantaged preschool children. *Child Development, 45*, 920–927.

Ross, H. S., & Kay, D. A. (1980). The origins of social play. In K. H. Rubin (Ed.), *New directions in child development: Children's play* (pp. 17–31). San Francisco: Jossey-Bass.

Rubenstein, J. (1976). Concordance of visual and manipulative responsiveness to novel and familiar stimuli: A function of test procedures or of prior experience? *Child Development, 47*, 1197–1199.

Rubenstein, J., & Howes, C. (1976). The effects of peers on toddler interaction with mothers and toys. *Child Development, 47*, 597–605.

Rubin, K. H. (1977). Play behaviors of young children. *Young Children, 32*(6), 16–24.

Rubin, K. H. (1980a). Editor's notes. In K. H. Rubin (Ed.), *New directions for child development: Children's play* (pp. vii–ix). San Francisco: Jossey-Bass.

Rubin, K. H. (1980b). Fantasy play: Its role in the development of social skills and social cognition. In K. H. Rubin (Ed.), *New directions in child development: Children's play* (pp. 69–84). San Francisco: Jossey-Bass.

Rubin, K. H. (1982a). Early play theories revisited: Contributions to contemporary research. In D. J. Pepler & K. H. Rubin (Eds.), *The play of children: Current theory and research*. Basel, Switzerland: Karger.

Rubin, K. H. (1982b). Nonsocial play in preschoolers: Necessarily evil? *Child Development, 53*, 651–657.

Rubin, K. H. (1985a). Play, peer interaction and social development. In C. C. Brown & A. W. Gottfried (Eds.), *Play interactions: The role of toys and parental involvement in children's development* (pp. 88–96). Skillman, NJ: Johnson & Johnson.

Rubin, K. H. (1985b). *The Play Observation Scale (POS)* (rev. ed.). Available from K. H. Rubin, University of Waterloo, Waterloo, Ontario, N2L 3G1, Canada.

Rubin, K. H., Fein, G. G., & Vandenberg, B. (1983). Play. In E. M. Hetherington (Ed.). P. H. Mussen (Series Ed.), *Handbook of child psychology: Vol. 4. Socialization, personality, and social development* (pp. 693–774). New York: Wiley.

Rubin, K. H., & Krasnor, R. (1986). Social-cognitive and behavioral perspectives on problem solving. In M. Perlmutter (Ed.), *Minnesota Symposia on Child Psychology* (Vol. 18). Hillsdale, NJ: Erlbaum.

Rubin, K. H., & Maioni, T. (1975). Play preference and its relationship to egocentrism, popularity and classification skills in preschoolers. *Merrill-Palmer Quarterly, 21*, 171–179.

Rubin, K. H., Maioni, T. L., & Hornung, H. (1976). Free play behaviors in middle and lower class preschoolers: Parten and Piaget revisited. *Child Development, 47*, 414–419.

Rubin, K. H., & Seibel, C. G. (1979, April). *The effects of ecological setting on the cognitive and social play behaviors of preschoolers.* Paper presented at the annual meeting of the American Educational Research Association, San Francisco.

Rubin, K. H., & Seibel, C. (1981, January). *The effects of ecological setting on the cognitive and social play behaviors of preschoolers.* Paper presented at the Annual International Inter-disciplinary Conference on Piagetian Theory and the Helping Professions, Los Angeles.

Rubin, K. H., Watson, K. S., & Jambor, T. W. (1978). Free-play behaviors in preschool and kindergarten children. *Child Development, 49*, 534–536.

Ruopp, R., Travers, J., Glantz, F., & Coelen, C. (1979). *Children at the center: Final results of the National Day Care Study.* Cambridge, MA: Abt Associates.

S

Sachs, J. (1980). The role of adult-child play in language development. In K. H. Rubin (Ed.), *New directions for child development: Children's play* (pp. 33–48). San Francisco: Jossey-Bass.

Saltz, E., Dixon, D., & Johnson, J. (1977). Training disadvantaged preschoolers on various fantasy activities: Effects on cognitive functioning and impulse control. *Child Development, 48*, 367–380.

Saltz, E., & Johnson, J. (1974). Training for thematic-fantasy play in culturally disadvantaged children: Preliminary results. *Journal of Educational Psychology, 66*, 623–630.

Sanders, K. M., & Harper, L. V. (1976). Free-play fantasy behavior in preschool children: Relations among gender, age, season, and location. *Child Development, 47*, 1182–1185.

Schirrmacher, R. (1986). Talking with young children about their art. *Young Children, 41* (5), 3–7.

Schwartzman, H. B. (1978). *Transformations: The anthropology of children's play.* New York: Plenum.

Schwartzman, H. B. (1979). The sociocultural context of play. In B. Sutton-Smith (Ed.), *Play and learning* (pp. 239–255). New York: Gardner.

Schwartzman, H. B. (1984). Imaginative play: Deficit or difference? In T. D. Yawkey & A. D. Pellegrini (Eds.), *Child's play: Developmental and applied* (pp. 49–62). Hillsdale, NJ: Erlbaum.

Schwartzman, H.B. (1985). Child-structured play: A cross-cultural perspective. In C. C. Brown & A. W. Gottfried (Eds.), *Play interactions: The role of toys and parental involvement in children's development* (pp. 11–19). Skillman, NJ: Johnson & Johnson.

Seligman, M. E. P., Peterson, C., Kaslow, N. J., Tanenbaum, R. L., Alloy, L. B., & Abramson, L. Y. (1984). Attributional style and depressive symptoms among children. *Journal of Abnormal Psychology, 93*, 235–238.

Serbin, L. A., & Connor, J. M. (1979, April). *Environmental control of sex related behaviors in the preschool*. Paper presented at the Biennial Meeting of the Society for Research in Child Development, San Francisco.

Serbin, L. A., Tonick, I. J., & Sternglanz, S. H. (1977). Shaping cooperative cross-sex play. *Child Development, 48*, 924–929.

Shapiro, S. (1975). Preschool ecology: A study of three environmental variables. *Reading Improvement, 12*, 236–241.

Shotwell, J. M., Wolf, D., & Gardner, H. (1979). Exploring early symbolization: Styles of achievement. In B. Sutton-Smith (Ed.), *Play and learning* (pp. 127–156). New York: Gardner.

Singer, D. G., & Rummo, J. (1973). Ideational creativity and behavior style in kindergarten aged children. *Developmental Psychology, 8*, 154–161.

Singer, D. G., & Singer, J. L. (1976). Family television viewing habits and the spontaneous play of preschool children. *American Journal of Orthopsychiatry, 46*, 496–502.

Singer, D. G., & Singer, J. L. (1979a). *Television viewing and aggressive behavior in preschool children: A field study*. Paper presented at the Conference on Forensic Psychology, New York.

Singer, J. L., & Singer, D. G. (1979b). The values of imagination. In B. Sutton-Smith (Ed.), *Play and learning* (pp. 195–218). New York: Gardner.

Smilansky, S. (1968). *The effects of sociodramatic play on disadvantaged preschool children*. New York: Wiley.

Smith, P. K. (1977). Social and fantasy play in young children. In B. Tizard & D. Harvey (Eds.), *Biology of play*. Philadelphia: Lippincott.

Smith, P. K. (1978). A longitudinal study of social participation in preschool children: Solitary and parallel play reexamined. *Developmental Psychology, 14*, 517–523.

Smith, P. K., & Connolly, K. J. (1972). Patterns of play and social interaction in preschool children. In N. B. Jones (Ed.), *Ethological studies of child behavior* (pp. 65–69). Cambridge, England: Cambridge University Press.

Smith, P. K., & Connolly, K. J. (1976). Social and aggressive behavior in preschool children as a function of crowding. *Social Science Information, 16*, 601–620.

Smith, P. K., & Connolly, K. J. (1980). *The ecology of preschool behavior*. Cambridge, England: Cambridge University Press.

Smith, P. K., Daglish, M., & Herzmark, G. (1981). A comparison of the effects of fantasy play tutoring and skills tutoring in nursery classes. *International Journal of Behavioral Development, 4*, 421–441.

Smith, P. K., & Dutton, S. (1979). Play training in direct and innovative problem-solving. *Child Development, 50*, 830–836.

Smith, P. K., & Green, M. (1975). Aggressive behavior in English nurseries and play groups: Sex differences and response of adults. *Child Development, 46*, 211–214.

Smith, P. K., & Syddall, S. (1978). Play and nonplay tutoring in preschool children: Is it play or tutoring which matters? *British Journal of Educational Psychology, 48*, 315–325.

Smith, P. K., & Vollstedt, R. (1985). On defining play: An empirical study of the relationship between play and various criteria. *Child Development, 56*, 1042–1050.

Stone, G. P. (1971). The play of little children. In R. E. Herron & B. Sutton-Smith (Eds.), *Child's play* (pp. 4–14). New York: Wiley.

Strom, R. D. (1981). Observing parent-child fantasy play. In R. D. Strom (Ed.), *Growing through play* (pp. 85–99). Belmont, CA: Brooks/Cole.

Sutton-Smith, B. (1968). Novel responses to toys. *Merrill-Palmer Quarterly, 14*, 151–158.

Sutton-Smith, B. (1979). Epilogue: Play as performance. In B. Sutton-Smith (Ed.), *Play and learning* (pp. 295–322). New York: Gardner.

Sutton-Smith, B. (1985). Origins and developmental processes of play. In C. C. Brown & A. W. Gottfried (Eds.), *Play interactions: The role of toys and parental involvement in children's development* (pp. 61–66). Skillman, NJ: Johnson & Johnson.

Sutton-Smith, B., & Kelly-Byrne, D. (1984). The idealization of play. In P. K. Smith (Ed.), *Play in animals and humans* (pp. 305–321). New York: Blackwell.

Sylva, K., Bruner, J. S., & Genova, P. (1976). The role of play in the problem-solving of children 3- to 5-years-of-age. In J. S. Bruner, A. Jolly, & K. Sylva (Eds.), *Play—Its role in development and evolution* (pp. 244–257). New York: Basic.

T

Tizard, B. (1977). Play: The child's way of learning? In B. Tizard & D. Harvey (Eds.), *Biology of play* (pp. 199–208). Philadelphia: Lippincott.

Tizard, B., Philps, J., & Plewis, I. (1976a). Play in pre-school centers—I. Play measures and their relation to age, sex, and IQ. *Journal of Child Psychology and Psychiatry and Allied Disciplines, 17*, 251–264.

Tizard, B., Philps, J., & Plewis, I. (1976b). Play in pre-school centers—II. Effects on play of the child's social class and of the educational orientation of the center. *Journal of Child Psychology and Psychiatry and Allied Disciplines, 17*, 265–274.

Trostle, S. L. (1984). Play therapy and the disruptive child. In T. D. Yawkey & A. D. Pellegrini (Eds.), *Child's play and play therapy* (pp. 157–169). Lancaster, PA: Technomic.

U

Ulvund, S. E. (1980). Cognition and motivation in early infancy: An interactionist approach. *Human Development, 23*, 17–32.

Ungerer, J., Zelazo, P. R., Kearsley, R. B., & O'Leary, K. (1981). Developmental changes in the representation of objects in symbolic play from 18 to 34 months of age. *Child Development, 52*, 186–195.

Uzgiris, I. (1976). Organization of sensorimotor intelligence. In M. Lewis (Ed.), *Origins of intelligence* (pp. 123–163). New York: Plenum.

Uzgiris, I. C., & Hunt, J. M. (1975). *Assessment in infancy*. Chicago: University of Illinois Press.

V

Vandell, D. L. (1977). *Boy toddlers' social interaction with mothers, fathers and peers.* Unpublished doctoral dissertation, Boston University.

Vandell, D. L., Wilson, K. S., & Buchanan, N. R. (1980). Peer interaction in the first year of life: An examination of its structure, content, and sensitivity to toys. *Child Development, 51,* 481–488.

Vandenberg, B. (1981a). Developmental features of children's play with objects. *The Journal of Psychology, 109,* 27–29.

Vandenberg, B. (1981b). The role of play in the development of insightful tool-using strategies. *Merrill-Palmer Quarterly, 27,* 97–109.

Vandenberg, B. (1985). Beyond the ethology of play. In C. C. Brown & A. W. Gottfried (Eds.), *Play interactions: The role of toys and parental involvement in children's development* (pp. 45–52). Skillman, NJ: Johnson & Johnson.

Vygotsky, L. S. (1967). Play and its role in the mental development of the child. *Soviet Psychology, 5*(3), 6–18.

W

Wachs, T. D. (1985). Home stimulation and cognitive development. In C. C. Brown & A. W. Gottfried (Eds.), *Play interaction: The role of toys and parental involvement in children's development* (pp. 142–152). Skillman, NJ: Johnson & Johnson.

Watson, J. S., & Ramey, C. T. (1972). Reactions to responses-contingent stimulation in early infancy. *Merrill-Palmer Quarterly, 18,* 219–227.

Watson, M. W., & Fischer, K. W. (1977). A developmental sequence of agent use in late infancy. *Child Development, 48,* 828–836.

Weisler, A., & McCall, R. B. (1976). Exploration and play: Resume and redirection. *American Psychologist, 31,* 492–508.

White, R. W. (1959). Motivation reconsidered: The concept of competence. *Psychological Review, 66,* 297–323.

Wilson, J. M. (1985). Play in the hospital. In C. C. Brown & A. W. Gottfried (Eds.), *Play interactions: The role of toys and parental involvement in children's development* (pp. 113–121). Skillman, NJ: Johnson & Johnson

Wolf, D. P. (1984). Repertoire, style and format: Notions worth borrowing from children's play. In P. K. Smith (Ed.), *Play in animals and humans* (pp. 175–193). New York: Blackwell.

Wolf, D., & Grollman, S. H. (1982). Ways of playing: Individual differences in imaginative style. In D. J. Pepler & K. H. Rubin (Eds.), *The play of children: Current theory and research* (pp. 46–63). Basel, Switzerland: Karger.

Y

Yarrow, L. J., Morgan, G. A., Jennings, K. D., Harmon, R. J., & Gaiter, J. L. (1982). Infants' persistence at tasks: Relationships to cognitive functioning and early experience. *Infant Behavior and Development, 5,* 131–141.

Index